10 Tools

for Applying Minimalism at Work

A Modest Tale of Tim's Quest for Freedom

Céleste Grimard

Copyright © 2019, 2023, 2025 Céleste Grimard.

All rights reserved.

This book and its contents are protected by copyright, including rights related to text and data mining, AI training, and similar technologies. No part of this publication may be reproduced, stored in a retrieval system, modified, or transmitted in any form or by any means – electronic, mechanical, or otherwise – without prior written permission from the author. The images were created by the author and enhanced by ChatGPT. Grammarly was used for proofreading. This book is fictional in nature. Any resemblance to individuals or events is coincidental.

ISBN: 978 1097478682

Acknowledgments

I sincerely thank David Hasell, Carmen Villadar, Philippe Alain, and Brenda Lee Lovell for their helpful comments on the first edition of this book. You have been a great sounding board! I also thank Joshua Fields Milburn and Ryan Nicodemus for their insights and contribution to minimalism. Finally, I thank all of the workers who have given me priceless insights into the world of work over many years.

Table of Contents

	Page
Foreword	3
Introduction	7
1 – Find your "Why"	13
2 – Create a Peaceful Workspace	19
3 – Simplify your Work Wardrobe	32
4 – Reduce Commuting Time	41
5 – Avoid Electronic Time Eaters	48
6 – Focus on the Vital Few	57
7 – Eliminate Mental Clutter	68
8 – Relax and Enjoy	87
9 – Eliminate People Clutter	100
10 – Put Work in Perspective	118
Final Thoughts	148
References	149

Foreword

Much has been written on minimalism as a way of life. Although many of the underlying principles of minimalism have existed under different incarnations (simplicity, essentialism, mindfulness, non-consumerism, frugal living, purpose-centered life, Zen, and many others), minimalists Joshua Fields Millburn and Ryan Nicodemus have drawn attention to it in a way that captured the attention of millions of people. Drawing from their personal experiences, they inspired people to want more – more meaning, more freedom, and more joy – and less *everything else*.

According to Joshua and Ryan, "Minimalism is a tool to rid yourself of life's excess in favor of focusing on what's important—so you can find happiness, fulfillment, and freedom."

Joshua and Ryan do a bang-up job of describing why and how to adopt minimalism in your personal lives. They escaped their corporate lives to find the freedom and time they needed to follow their passions. That's cool, but not all of us can step out of the corporate maze – or want to! Some of us really like our jobs despite feeling weighed down by them at times.

So, how do we practice minimalism at work? By doing the least amount of work possible? Nope! More than anything, **minimalism at work means working in a way that brings a sense of peace, meaning, and joy to your life.** Yes, this sounds like a lofty goal. So many workplaces are filled with stress, conflict, massive workloads, political maneuvering, back-biting competition, frenziness, hassles, ambiguities, and other stuff best described as 'general bullsh*t.'

Depending on your position, there may be things that you can't change or control. But there's a lot that you can do to make a difference at work. There may be things or ways of doing things that you take for granted that you can change if you get the ball rolling.

By way of a tale, this book focuses on a core set of actions that will help you adopt minimalism at work. This tale introduces you to two characters who work in the same office: Tim, who feels weighed down by his job, and Roxanne, who helps Tim lighten his load through 10 practical tools.

You might quibble with some of Roxanne's tips, but that's okay. We each have our own way of doing minimalism. Pick and choose what will make a difference for you. And don't worry: if your workplace isn't an office, you can still use the tools. Adapt them so that they work for you.

To keep this book brief, I've stuck to what I consider to be the essentials. There's a lot more that can be said, but then it wouldn't be much of a 'minimalist' book.

Enjoy your journey!

Introduction

Once upon a time, there lived a cool guy named Tim who worked in an office building with many other cool folks deep in the heart of Bridge City. When he was at work, Tim felt the weight of a growing load of bricks on his shoulders and, when he got home, the load was still there. Tim noticed that many other folks had bricks on their shoulders as well. "I can't wait until I retire. I'll be able to get rid of these bricks," he said, "They must come with the job."

Tim was plain old tired. "Blah," he would say to himself every morning while having his oatmeal and coffee before heading out to work. Fighting through traffic, Tim would arrive at his desk and face a different kind of rat race. Tim's work was busy, stressful, taxing. Tim had too much to do, and there were lots of hassles, pressure to get more done, and general struggles to stay on top of everything. Every day was the same – he would wake up, go to work, work without ever feeling like he was making headway, and then return home exhausted.

One day, Roxanne moved into the office next to Tim's. Roxanne was doing the same kind of work as Tim, but Tim noticed that Roxanne didn't have any bricks on her back. Tim figured that the bricks would show up sooner or later, but they didn't. And there was more. Roxanne seemed to enjoy her work: she had all her ducks in a row, and there was something else that he just couldn't quite put his finger on — a sense of peacefulness and joy radiating from Roxanne and her office. He couldn't figure it out. Especially when he looked at his own office...

One day, while curiously looking around Roxanne's office for signs of bricks tucked away somewhere but finding none, Tim asked, "Hey, Roxanne, where did you hide your bricks?"

Roxanne smiled and said, "In my last job, I carried lots of bricks on my back, just like you're doing right now. It was only when I nearly broke my back that I realized that I needed to do something – anything – different."

"What?" Tim replied in disbelief, "You can't get rid of the bricks. They come with the job. Everyone's got 'em!"

"Hey, I had them, too, but a friend wheedled me into going to a talk by two minimalists, Joshua Fields Millburn and Ryan Nicodemus, one evening at Amigos Cantina," she continued, "I went for the nachos and beer, but I left realizing that I was stuck on a hamster wheel of my own making. I had never taken the time to ask myself if what I was doing was working for me. Changing metaphors now, I had gotten used to the bricks and commiserating with my buddies about how heavy they were. So I asked myself some serious questions about whether I REALLY wanted to get rid of them. Like you said, everybody's got bricks; it's almost fashionable to complain about them. They're like a badge of honor. The more bricks, the better, it seems. But, you know, they weigh us down in ways that we don't even realize until they're gone. Once I got rid of them, I realized not only how heavy they were but, sadly, that I could have gotten rid of them a long time ago."

"Hey, I absolutely want to get rid of these bricks and I don't want to wait till I retire, but I don't know how."

"Well, over time, I found some tools for chipping away at the bricks. It wasn't easy, but with a lot of trial and error and step-by-step, I transformed my life at work."

"Cool. Where do I start? And can I borrow those tools stat?" Tim excitedly begged Roxanne, imagining that she had a masonry chisel, pickaxe, a mallet, and other such tools.

"I'll give you my whole toolbox, Tim," Roxanne replied as she reached behind her desk and pulled out a worn-out toolbox. Tim briskly opened the toolbox but was bewildered when he saw that it contained only paper.

"What's this?" Tim was perplexed, "Paper? You've gotta be kidding! I need something heavy-duty."

"You'll see," Roxanne chuckled as Tim left her office with the toolbox in hand.

~~~

Back in his office, Tim slouched in his office chair. He was seriously disappointed; he wanted to knock off the bricks with the blunt force of a gigantic mallet — once and for all, quickly and easily — and then get right back to work. Sigh! After shoving the toolbox into the corner of his office, he dragged himself to the coffee shop to commiserate with his brick-laden coworkers.

Many days went by (imagine the day sheets on his desk calendar flying into the air), and Tim noticed that he was carrying even more bricks than ever on his back. Meanwhile, Roxanne's back was still free of

> "If you have to buy stuff to store your stuff, you might have too much stuff."
> —becomingminimalist.com

bricks. "If I don't do something, I'll have so many bricks on my back that I won't be able to walk," Tim sighed. "Hmm, what's the worst that can happen?" he asked himself as he spied the dusty toolbox in the corner of his office, covered with papers and files. He dug it out, opened the lid, and saw the paper. Sigh!

Clutching the top papers in the pile in his hands, he glanced at Roxanne's handwritten notes.

"Ah…" Tim said to himself, shaking his head, "10 tips and no quick fix. Too much work. I'll get started another day. Besides, things aren't that bad, and I like all my stuff. And isn't it normal to have a messy office and be unhappy at work?" So, Tim flung the papers on top of the open toolkit and dragged himself to the coffee shop to commiserate with his brick-laden coworkers (again).

Once back from the coffee shop, Tim looked around his messy, stuffed office and muttered to himself, "Well, maybe it's just a matter of organizing things. You know, there are tons of shows about organizing stuff. That must be the ticket." So, in a burst of energy, Tim bought special containers for storing stuff and a high-tech labeler, and he shoveled stuff into containers and bins and drawers. It was tons of work, but Tim felt satisfied when he saw that everything was in matching, see-through plastic containers with neat, color-coded labels.

On Tim's shelves were containers full of files, magazines, papers, expense statements, client documents, office paper, envelopes, pens, and several bins labeled 'miscellaneous.' His office supplies were in separate containers depending on their function. For example, everything that 'attached' was in one container: glue sticks, staples, tape,

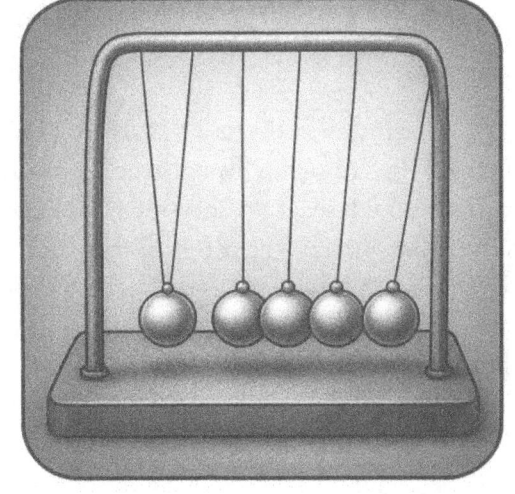

and paper clips. Everything that 'wrote' was in another container: pens, markers, pencils, and highlighters. Everything that was 'paper' was in another container: small note pads, post-its, and 8 x 11½ lined paper. His filing cabinets were full of files that he left untouched. His dusty book collection continued to fill dozens of shelves around his office. And his many knick-knacks (baseball bobble-heads, framed pictures, postcards from Chicago, old coffee cups, Newton's cradle balance balls, stress balls, and other tchotchkes picked up at conventions) were collecting dust on the shelves in front of his books.

There was still lots of stuff in Tim's office, but some of it was organized. It had taken an enormous amount of time and energy. Still, now Tim could see the floor of his office and the (few) parts of his desktop that weren't covered with project binders, documents, pens, and yesterday's lunch. Tim sat back in his chair and admired the fruits of his labor. "Ah! It wasn't that hard after all," Tim said to himself, feeling triumphant. All was good. Or was it?

1

Find your "Why"

Despite all his effort, the bricks were still weighing down on Tim's back. Tim enjoyed the 'look' of his office, but, to be honest, there was still stuff in every nook and cranny. The only difference was that some of it was in containers. Containers that he had to search every time he needed a particular file. Dozens of containers that he bumped into when he tried to get to his desk. Alas, Tim's attempt to organize his space didn't bring him any lasting relief. After a couple of weeks, he dejectedly stopped in at Roxanne's office.

"How are the tools working for you, Tim?" Roxanne asked.

"Well, I made a big effort to organize my office. You know, put all the stuff in containers. It was a ton of work, and it actually looks good, but I have to admit that I don't feel any different," Tim replied, feeling the pinch of the many bricks on his back.

> **The Organizing Trap**
>
> Thinking that putting stuff in labeled bins will bring you peace.

"I'm sorry to hear that, Tim," Roxanne said, "You've fallen into The Organizing Trap. You've organized your stuff, but you've still got the stuff. It may not look like clutter, but it still feels that way, and it's weighing you down! As Joshua and Ryan say, 'Organizing is the same as well-planned hoarding.' It doesn't get you far. You know, minimalism isn't just about organizing your stuff, and it's not even just about getting rid of it. The core of it is much bigger than that. Sure, it's partly about stuff, but it's also about looking at yourself. For me, minimalism means focusing on having more meaning, freedom, and joy in my life and less *everything else*. SO, I try to minimize or get rid of anything that doesn't bring meaning, freedom, and joy in my life."

"Yeah, I guess, but, you know, I read the first pages in the box. It was good food for thought, but I didn't quite know what to do next," Tim said.

"Ah, the stuff on those pages is meant to get you in the spirit of minimalism and get you thinking about why it might be of value to you. If you know why you want to do something, then you're more likely to make an effort to do it and stick with it. When the going gets tough, your 'whys' will help to pull you through," Roxanne replied, "Let's go through the Tool 1 sheets together."

> **FIRST FIGURE OUT WHY.**
>
> **THEN HOW.**

~ ~ ~

So, for the next minutes, Tim and Roxanne discussed her notes for Tool 1 and why he might want to adopt minimalism at work. Tim was a tad bit despondent – all that work for nothing! But, Roxanne reassured him that the sorting that he did would be of some use. Tim took out a pad of paper, jotted down his 'whys', and committed to re-reading them as he applied the tools to his job. Knowing that he might be rid of the bricks one day, he felt a massive sense of relief. And a brick slid off his back…

Tim's "whys"

Get those bricks off my back. Feel stress-free when I enter my office and spend time in there. Streamline my work. Make more work life less stressful and more peaceful. Focus on what's important and what brings value and let go of the rest. Get more meaning, peace, freedom, and joy in my life. So I can breathe.

Tool 1 – Find your "Why"

WHY do you want to adopt minimalism at work? What's your motivation?

Joshua & Ryan say that "Minimalism is *a tool to rid yourself of life's excess in favor of focusing on what's important — so you can find happiness, fulfillment, and freedom.*" So cool!

→ Purge life's excess = too much stuff, too many commitments, how we complexify our lives, just plain too much! Excess = distraction from what's most important!

→ Focus = simplify, get rid of, let go, and figure out what's important! Why waste your time on what won't make a difference?

→ Find meaning, joy, peace, and freedom NOW. Now is a good time. If not, when? Why wait?

   → Does any of this resonate with you? What is YOUR why?

Johanna Jansen's principles from her website

→ "Minimalism is simplifying space, routines, schedules, and commitments to live a calmer and more mindful life."

→ "Minimalism is eliminating all the excess in possessions, commitments, and relationships, to increase focus on what really matters and start adding value to your world."

→ "Minimalism is aiming for detachment from possessions, ego, and status to make yourself less vulnerable and more flexible to adapt to whatever life has to offer."

→ How about you?
→ Do you want to simplify, eliminate, and detach?

In a nutshell...

- Less stuff means more freedom.
- Stockpiles of stuff 'just in case you need them' are rooted in fear and insecurity.
- Simplicity yields clarity.
- Stuff gets in the way of your focusing on what is important.
- Stuff takes time to manage and comb through when you're trying to find what you actually need.
- Life gets lived in the moment. Let go and live.

🕯 Happiness can't be found in stuff.

🕯 Find what brings value to you and focus on that.

Stuff = physical stuff, routines, schedules, commitments, relationships, ways of thinking, ego, status

→ Does any of this resonate with you?

2

Create a peaceful workspace

Now that he knew WHY he wanted to apply minimalism to his work, Tim was ready to know HOW to make it happen. So, he grabbed the next pages, looked at the title, and ran into Roxanne's office. "Okay, so now it's all about decluttering and organizing my office, which I've already done. So, I'll move on to the next step, right?"

"Well, yes, it is about your workspace. First, you need to make decisions about what to keep, how to keep it, and what to do with the rest. Organizing is what you do with what's left in the office. You don't have to organize the stuff you're not going to keep."

"Shoot! Did I do all that work for nothing?"

"Tim, it sounds like you sorted some of your stuff into categories, and that'll help you with this tool. This tool is a big ask. In fact, it's what people normally associate with minimalism — dealing with the stuff that you see around you. But it is doable — one step at a time."

> **LESS STUFF
> = MORE VISUAL PEACE
> + BREATHING ROOM
> + LESS TIME
> WASTED LOOKING
> FOR THINGS
> + MORE PRODUCTIVITY**

"I'll give it a whirl. I'll do anything to get those bricks off my back."

"It's probably best to start at the top of my list of tips — office supplies - and work your way to the bottom because you're less likely to be attached to stuff such as office supplies. So, pull out all your containers of office supplies. You might be surprised by how many office supplies you accumulate over time — a pen here, a pad of paper there, and you've got a drawer of 20 miscellaneous pens, five pencils, eight markers, six highlighters, 12 pads of paper, and other doodads (some of which aren't working or you just aren't using). If you keep all this stuff, your office could end up looking like a supply cabinet."

"That's right. Not to mention that I inherited tons of miscellaneous stuff that the last guy left in the office. But, hey, some people ARE attached to their office supplies. Take Milton from *Office Space*, for example, who loved his red stapler. That red stapler was the only special thing he had, and it brought him a bit of joy. Besides, I've already organized all my office supplies into containers. I have at least three bins full! Done!"

"That's a massive stockpile of office supplies, Tim. Do you really use all of them?"

"Well, no, not right now, but I might need them in the future. You never know, eh? I don't want to be stuck one day without a highlighter. Besides, I'm not about to ask myself those Six Key Questions in Tool 2 for every single item. That would be tedious."

"Don't go *through* your stockpile, Tim. For your office supplies, just pull out what you currently use and one spare: so, one pen and one spare pen, one highlighter, and one spare highlighter, etc. That's it. Put the rest (whatever's useable) in a box and, if you can't return them to the department's supply cabinet or otherwise get rid of the stuff inside the organization, donate it."

> **Joshua and Ryan's 20/20 rule:**
> Get rid of just-in-case items if you can replace them in under $20.

"What do you mean by *currently use?*" I haven't used an interoffice envelope in six months, but I might need it one day."

> **80/20 rule:**
> We use 20% of our stuff. So why not get rid of the rest?

"I only have enough office supplies to meet my current needs, or that wouldn't put me in a bind if I ran out. It was a challenge for me, but I eliminated all the things that I was holding onto 'just in case' I needed them if I hadn't used them in the last 90 days. The department's supply cabinet is close by, you know. You don't need to stockpile stuff."

"True enough. I guess I can let go of some of my stuff. It'll be hard to let go of my books, though. I have to admit that I haven't read half of them. They sounded interesting, but I just didn't get around to reading them, and, quite frankly, I don't know when I will have the time to read them. But I might need them one day. You never know!"

"Believe it or not, I used to have a couple of thousand books myself. So, I understand your attachment to your books. Somehow, I thought that having these books was the same as knowing what was in them or that I would look really smart and well-read, and I had every good intention of reading them.

> Joshua and Ryan's 90/90 rule:
>
> Get rid of whatever you haven't used in the past 90 days and don't expect to use in the next 90 days.

But, and this might sound ridiculous, one day, I decided to get rid of an entire shelving unit full of books, so, for each book, I asked myself if I would buy this book if I didn't already have it, and I was surprised by the number of books that I got rid of – more than a thousand. I gave some to coworkers, I put some on the lunch table with a "free books" note, and I sent some to family, libraries, hospitals for their patient reading library, and second-hand stores. I left some on the benches with a note indicating that they're free for whoever wants them. It was a win-win situation. These folks were happy, and I was free of these books. I haven't missed them, and, since then, I've been gradually giving away more books. Yes, even books I received as gifts. And I mainly read e-books or borrow them from the library instead of buying them now. When I do buy a book, I take one off my shelf and give it away (one in, one out). Professional organizer Andrew Mellon calls this Stuff Equilibrium. Also, I'm working my way to having only two shelves to house all of my books; so, there's a physical limit to how many books I can have."

"That sounds good, Roxanne. I caught a glimpse of the *Tidying Up with Marie Kondo* show on Netflix while looking for a good show to watch. Apparently, I should hold a book or whatever in my hands and, without opening it, ask myself if it brings me joy. But, to be truthful, there's nothing in my office that sparks joy, except the picture of my family, of

> **STUFF EQUILIBIRIUM**
>
> HAVING ENOUGH OF EVERYTHING THAT SERVES YOU AND NOTHING THAT DOESN'T.
>
> (ANDREW MELLON)

course. Anyhow, there are maybe a dozen books that resonate with me. You know what I mean?"

"Sure. There's a graphic novel called *Thoreau at Walden* by John Porcellino that I absolutely love. It's beautifully written and simply illustrated, and it reminds me of what's important in life. I read it and re-read it. If I were stranded on a desert island and could only bring a few books with me, this would be one of them."

"Point made. Those are good questions to ask myself:
→ Would I buy this book if I didn't already have it?
→ Do I plan to read it in the next six months?
→ Can I read it at the library?
→ Are digital versions available?
→ Does the book *speak* to me?
→ Would I bring it with me to a desert island?
→ If I only have two shelves for books, which books would I keep?
In other words, I should limit the amount of space that I allow for my books (and other things, too). Okay, that takes care of books, but my office is full of paper and files. I've already organized them, but they're still there, and I'm back to drowning in a sea of paper."

"I was drowning in a mess of paperwork, too, till I scanned every piece of paper that was in my office and that came into my office (only those that I needed, of course). Instead of *processing* paper, I do most of my work electronically (and, in person, of course). My clients were more than happy to oblige. I looked up the company's record management policies, and I was able to shred many of the paper files or send them to the central archives. I still have some paper copies of documents filed in folders in alpha order, but very few."

"Yikes. What if your hard drive crashes, and you lose all those documents?"

"Well, of course, I keep several backups – here on our workplace network, an external hard drive, etc. – whatever's allowed by the company. Make sure that you check with the record management folks about handling your paperwork – what needs to be kept in its original form, what needs to be shredded, and what can just be recycled. Oh, I should mention that, at first, it was hard for me to stop printing documents to read them. But, after a few weeks, I realized that it was just as easy to read the documents on my computer. I just needed to form a new habit."

"I noticed that the tool says to get rid of my knick-knacks and decorative items. What gives? I like personalizing my office and surrounding myself with things I like, such as my collection of bobblehead baseball players. Besides, it tells people who I am and gives them a conversation starter. All work and no play makes Tim look like a dull boy, don't you think? I don't want my office to look sterile. And all my postcards from my travels and the little doodads, stress balls, and gadgets that I picked up at conventions are fun. They remind me of fun times. They show that I'm a cool, well-traveled person. Don't they?"

"You can answer your own question, Tim. The idea is that these things come with a cost. They take space, time, and focus away from your work, even though you may not realize it. However cool they are, they distract you – even momentarily – from your work. Anyhow, I suggest that you try an experiment – take all of these things (except for the picture of your family, of course, since it brings you joy) and box them. Put the box in a place where you can't see it. After six months or so, ask yourself if you really missed any of these things, if you're more focused on your work, and if you're less approachable or interesting because they're not around."

"Letting go of my attachment to things – that seems to be the message. It's hard because I'm so used to being surrounded by stuff. But, hey, I can do as much or as little of it as I want, and I can take my time doing it. No one's got a gun to my head…just bricks on my back! About the other stuff, I keep a coffee cup on my desk, but very few personal items. You know, Joe next door, he has several changes of clothes, a gym bag, a pickleball racket, four pairs of shoes, and other stuff. People wonder if he lives in his office, and –"

"What Joe does is his business. I, myself, have a couple of pairs of shoes here, but I keep them in a box on the lowest shelf. I don't want my office to look like a closet, so any personal items are out of sight."

"I noticed that. Also, you don't seem to have much furniture in your office. Is more on its way, Roxanne?"

"You know, Tim, when I moved here, my office was empty, and I was allowed to choose my furniture. Usually, people get what's already in their offices. Anyhow, I have all that I need. If I have more shelving or filing units, I'll just be tempted to fill them up. What's that expression: work expands to fill the time available? Well, I think that stuff expands to fill the space available. The more space I have available for stuff, the more stuff I will put in that space. You know, I had a huge condo a few years back, and I filled every room with furniture and random stuff. Decorating was fun, but the upkeep and cleaning of the stuff (not to mention the fact that I didn't use most of the stuff) was draining."

"Oh, I can see that. And I bet that you didn't use most of the rooms. My family rarely uses the formal dining room. The place sits empty except for 2 or 3 days of the year. What a waste…"

"I agree. Anyhow, getting back to the office, here on my desktop, I keep just what I'm working on right now. Otherwise, I'm distracted when I see the other files out of the corner of my eye. Clutter's distracting effect has been proven by neuroscientists. In Stephanie McMains and Sabine Kastner's research, when people worked in a cluttered room, they were distracted and unable to focus or think straight. Those who worked in an uncluttered space had significantly higher levels of concentration, productivity, and focused thinking."

"Hmm…no wonder…"

"What about your office, Tim? Is your desktop full of papers, knick-knacks, office supplies, and other random objects? Is there any furniture that you could get rid of? If you had to start fresh, what would your office look like? How would you organize it? Don't just assume that you can't make changes, Tim."

"Well, I definitely have some work to do to clean my desktop and make my office functional. I usually have files on the floor and the visitors' chairs. You know, I always thought that I should keep my office looking full of papers with lots of post-it notes on my desk, etc. so that my boss and others would get the impression that I'm super busy and not give me extra work. ("How's that working for you?") And, hey, my boss has commented on my busyness in the past, so it's kind of working. I'm a bit scared that an immaculate, neat, sparse-looking office like yours may give the impression that I'm not working or that I don't have enough to do."

"We have the same boss, Tim, so that doesn't really fly with me. But I understand what you're saying. In a sense, it has become so common to hear people saying that they're overloaded and busy and stressed that it's an automatic thing to hear. If you say that all is cool, that you're not stressed, etc., then people might think that you're not working hard, or they might wonder what's up with you. In any case, the results speak for themselves. The hardest part is getting started, Tim. The idea is to minimize the stuff that will distract you and to simplify everything."

"Sounds good, Roxanne. I'm wondering if it's best to do this a little bit at a time."

"Go at your own pace, Tim, but here's a plug for doing it all at once. In their podcast called *Excess*, Ryan and Joshua say that getting rid of excess bit by bit is like removing a band-aid a little at a time: vvvvvery painful. That's food for thought."

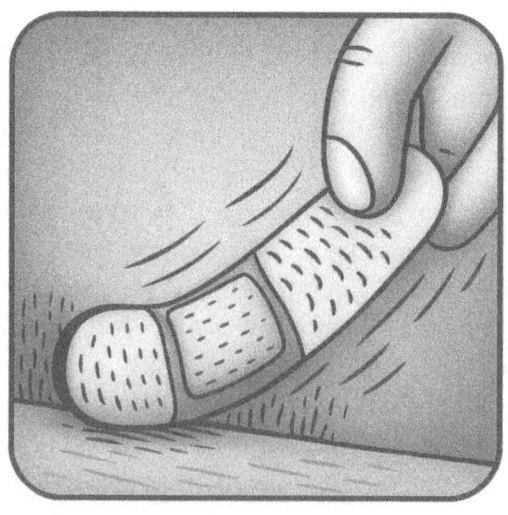

~ ~ ~

And with that, Tim sauntered back to his office feeling more encouraged but daunted by the work ahead of him. There were false starts and hesitations, but also small successes. Gradually, Tim began to feel disencumbered and that he could finally breathe in his office. Over time, he realized that he didn't need or really care for much of the stuff that he had hung on to. He felt better able to focus on his work… and, once again, a brick slid off his back.

Tool 2 –Create a Peaceful Workspace

"Most of us say yes to too much stuff, and then we let these little, mediocre things fill our lives." – Derek Sivers

"When your work environment is messy, there is often chaos in your mind. Tidy up your immediate work environment, and you will see order show up in your life!" – Paul Rousseau (translated from French)

"Clutter is the physical manifestation of unmade decisions fueled by procrastination." – Christina Scalese

"Things accumulate in large part because people procrastinate, putting off decisions as long as possible (sometimes indefinitely)." – Stephanie Culp

"That which you cannot give away, you do not possess. It possesses you." – Ivern Ball

The ability to simplify means eliminating the unnecessary so that the necessary may speak. — Hans Hoffman

Detach ~ Eliminate ~ Simplify ~ Keep

- ☑ Detach yourself from your stuff.
- ☑ Eliminate everything that doesn't add value or help you be productive.
- ☑ Eliminate or hide from view anything that distracts you from your work.
- ☑ Simplify your office set-up. Have 'a place for everything and everything in its place.' Keep 'like items' together. Keep frequently used items close by. Put things back where they belong.
- ☑ Keep only what is necessary, useful, and important to you right now.

Six Key Questions

For EVERYTHING in your office (office supplies, books and manuals, papers and files, knick-knacks and other miscellaneous items; coffee cups, clothes, coats, shoes, and other personal items; office furniture, and other stuff), ask yourself:

1. When did I last use this?
2. Do I need this?
3. What would happen if I didn't have it?
4. Does this need to be in my office, or would it have a better home elsewhere?
5. Is this adding value to my work or helping me make a contribution?
6. Does this item increase my sense of peace, comfort, and joy?

Tool 2 – Roxanne's Tips

1. Office supplies – Keep 'one and a spare' of items that you have used in the past six months. Put the rest in a box and give it away.

2. Books and manuals – Keep those that are absolutely necessary for your work and that you would have trouble replacing if needed. For the remaining books, pick out a limited number of additional books that are significant to you [you be the judge, I found that 20 worked for me]. Designate a space of books and only keep the number of books that will fit in this space. Use the "one in, one out" principle if you're planning to add books. Give away any books that you haven't accessed in the past year and that you don't expect to read in the upcoming year to colleagues or others.

3. Papers and files – Depending on your office's record retention policies, sort and make decisions on paper files. Keep those that you need to do your day-to-day job. Some may need to go to a central filing room or other individuals. Some you can scan and then throw away or shred the original. And for some, the original document must be kept, but not necessarily in your office.

4. Tchotchkes, knick-knacks, postcards, decorative items, left-over take-out forks, and other miscellaneous items – Give away all of these or donate, recycle, or throw them out. Minimize the number of pictures and other 'items' that you have on the wall, shelves, or other surfaces. If the thought of doing this is difficult for you, put them all in a box and place the box out of sight. Re-evaluate what to keep after six months.

5. Coffee cups, clothes, coats, shoes, and other personal items – Keep one coffee cup/water bottle, your coat, and only a few personal items that you need in case of emergencies. Keep these out of sight if possible.

6. Office furniture – Ask yourself what your ideal workspace would look like and try to make it happen. If this is a decision that you're authorized to

make, keep only the furniture that you're actively using, plus a chair for a guest. Remove all extra chairs, empty filing cabinets, and shelving units. Don't be afraid to ask to have the excess furniture removed from your office. This is usually possible!

7. Desktop –Remove everything from your desktop. Then, only place on your desktop what you're currently using so that you can focus on what you're doing. Keep handy the things you use most often.

8. Follow organizers' rules:
    a. Like with like: Keep 'like' things together, for example, all office supplies together.
    b. Have a place for everything and put everything in its place. Return things to their place after using them.
    c. Designate a space for particular items, for example, books, and limit your collection to that space. Don't buy another bookcase, however tempting!
    d. Replace rather than add: When you acquire something new, replace it with something you already have. So, when you get a new coffee cup, for example, remove one that you're already using. This will prevent you from stockpiling duplicates of stuff.

9. At the end of every workday, take 10 minutes to put away stuff and clean and organize your office so that you can start the next day fresh.

3

Simplify your work wardrobe

Despite Tim's progress, other bricks were wedged on his back. It seems that minimizing the stuff around him brought him some morsels of peace, but there was more to do. Tim grabbed the next pages from the toolbox and knocked on Roxanne's door.

"Hey, Roxanne. Got a minute? I'm confused."

"Sure, come on in. What's up?"

"Well, I thought I had mastered minimalism; that it was all about my office, you know, DESK: Detach ~ Eliminate ~ Simplify ~

Keep. But there's a bunch more sheets of paper in the toolbox. And what's this about simplifying my wardrobe? Is that Tool 3?"

"Folks often associate minimalism with getting rid of stuff, but it's much more than that. It's a whole approach to life, looking not only at the physical stuff but everything else, including you. And simplifying your work wardrobe is another element of this process. Tim, have you noticed anything about what I wear to work?"

"Not really, no. You seem to be dressed professionally, but that's about all I could say. It seems weird to be talking about clothes. It's so personal."

"Tim, the idea behind this tool is to minimize the time and energy that it takes to get dressed for work while still looking professional. Believe it or not, every morning, some people, yes, even men, agonize over what to wear to work. They have a closet full of clothes, which gives them so many choices that they feel stressed and can't make a decision. Having a capsule wardrobe of five outfits takes the stress out of the decision. What to wear to work becomes a decision that you have already made before you have to get dressed, so getting dressed is quick and easy."

"Some people like to change up what they wear at work. It's part of their self-expression. Do you want to restrict what people wear? That's boring."

"Well, Tim, there's no obligation to use every tool in the toolbox, but give this a shot, you might like it. I used to be a clothes horse – I had two closets – well-organized ones – that were packed tight with clothes, shoes, purses, and more shoes. I had lots of options, but deciding what to wear became a pain in the *ss. I would try on clothes, then switch them when they didn't look good. I had lots of clothes but nothing to wear! Oh, and I had lots of 'disposable clothes.' Clothes that were too cheap to pass up. The sales were great, and I liked the clothes well enough (before they got used up, which happened quickly), but I had a motley crew of clothes, and nothing seemed to work together. And half my closet was filled with clothes that didn't really fit me (but that I hoped to fit into once I lost 20 pounds). I did 'aspirational' shopping: I bought stuff that I loved in a smaller size, hoping to fit into it one day. I watched shows and read books about what to wear and what not to wear, and how to create a stylish wardrobe. I sorted, organized, and gave away tons of clothes or put them on consignment. But I kept buying stuff, so the process kept repeating itself."

"Sounds like a costly mess. If you buy 10 shirts on sale, but don't wear any of them regularly, they're actually quite pricey."

"You're not kidding. The first thing I did was call a personal moratorium on buying clothes. This was hard to do because I considered shopping to be a form of entertainment or even retail therapy. But the more I exposed myself to stores, the more clothes I bought. So, I didn't go shopping. I had to stop the inflow of clothes so that I could really evaluate what I had. Then, I came across this website called Project333 that challenged people to wear only 33 items of clothing over three months."

"Did you try this experiment?"

"In my personal life, I experimented with wearing 20 clothing items (not all at the same time and not including gym clothes), and I found that it worked quite well. And no one said anything or seemed to notice. And then on Joshua Becker's blog, I read about how most women have 30 outfits, but that lots of successful people adopt a work uniform – a wardrobe made up of the same or similar items – as a way of simplifying their lives. It becomes one less decision for them to make. This frees up their mind and energy for more important things. So, I experimented with 10 outfits, but I found that it was too many. Five outfits and one pair of work shoes were just right."

"I don't know… I would feel self-conscious. What if someone notices that I wore the same shirt the previous week?"

"Oh, I get it. When I first started the experiment, I was VERY self-conscious. I thought that people would notice my limited wardrobe, but no one said anything. By the way, did you hear about the experiment that Richard Stewart, the mayor of Coquitlam, B.C., did? He wore the same blue suit for over 15 months in a row, and no one noticed! Anyhow, my clothes and shoes are professional and clean, and they suit me well. They're basically a non-issue. I don't have to worry about them, fiddle with them, or try to impress people with my huge wardrobe."

"But sometimes it's fun to dress up and have people compliment me for my nice bowtie or something. And there are lots of sayings about clothes, you know, 'Clothes make the man,' or 'Dress for success.' And the entire fashion industry and fashion magazines with new trends and styles can't be wrong."

"Well, first of all, you ARE dressing for success when you're wearing professional clothes that you feel great in and that suit you. Second, let's be clear about this: the fashion industry wants you to continue buying clothes. It's not going to encourage you to never buy clothes again!"

"I don't have to wear the same five outfits for an eternity, do I?"

"Nope. You can change them up. A friend of mine reviews her wardrobe and adds or subtracts stuff at the beginning of every season. The Tool is just a guideline; use it as you wish in a way that reduces your decision-making stress level."

"I can't say that I'm stressed about clothes."

"Hey, I didn't think that I was either. But when I started wearing my uniform (in other words, the five-outfit capsule), I realized how much simpler the day was when it started with one less decision to make."

~ ~ ~

And with that, Tim went back to his office feeling hesitant about using this Tool. He decided to do a Google search of 'wearing the same clothes every day.' There were lots of results, and he read about successful people such as Mark Zuckerberg who choose to wear a uniform so that they have one less decision to make.

That very evening, Tim opened his overstuffed closet doors. Whoosh! So many clothes!

He started his culling process by pulling out his bowtie collection. Where to start? Tim identified his favorite bowties and other work clothes – the ones that made him feel fabulous yet look professional and creative – and he created five capsule outfits.

Then, he packed the rest of his work clothes in garment bags and hung them in a closet in the guest bedroom. He was surprised by how easy this step was. By focusing on what he liked the most rather than on what to eliminate (and knowing that he could still access his other clothes if needed), he managed to streamline his work wardrobe in under an hour.

Unlike Roxanne, who mixed and matched individual items (thus, for example, wearing her pair of black pants twice in a week), Tim prepared five outfits with no 'overlapping' items: each outfit was complete. Moreover, Tim packed up all of his white or light-colored shirts. This would allow him to wash all of his shirts in one load, rather than having a separate load for whites/lights.

The next workday, Monday, Tim wore his first capsule outfit. And then he wore the other capsule outfits on the following days. The following Monday, Tim was a bit self-conscious, hoping no one would notice that he was wearing the same outfit as the previous Wednesday. But no one seemed to notice Tim's wardrobe choices.

Over time, Tim began to enjoy not having decisions to make about clothes in the morning. He just chose the next outfit that was hanging in his closet. Done! Getting dressed took less time and effort than in the past, and he still looked marvelous. One day, while admiring himself in the mirror, Tim noticed that one more brick had disappeared from his back. Fabulous!

Tool 3 – Simplify your Work Wardrobe

"One less frivolous decision in the morning leads to better decisions on things that really matter." –Joshua Becker

"Buy less, choose well & make it last." –Vivienne Westwood

"Simplicity is the key note of all true elegance." –Coco Chanel

"You'll never find something to wear that makes you feel beautiful, smart, or loved if you don't believe that you already are." –Project333

"Don't be into trends. Don't make fashion own you, but you decide what you are, what you want to express by the way you dress and the way to live." —Gianni Versace

Capsule ~ Professional ~ Simplify ~ Save

- ☑ Create a professional capsule wardrobe.
- ☑ Simplify your decision-making when getting dressed.
- ☑ Save expenses, time, energy, and stress.
- ☑ Get rid of excess.

From ALL YOUR WORK CLOTHES, create five different outfits that:
- ☑ Fit well and don't require repairs.
- ☑ Make you feel and look great.

- ☑ Would be considered professional work attire.
- ☑ Are simple and easy to wash.
- ☑ Can be mixed and matched, if desired.

Tool 3 –Roxanne's Tips

1. Separate your work clothes from the clothes that you wear in your personal life (unless you wear the same clothes at work and home).

2. Find three words that describe how you want to look at work. I use the word 'professional' because that's important to me. Here are some examples of other words: creative, smart, powerful, approachable, fun, neat, etc.

3. From all your work clothes, create five complete outfits that fit with your three words from #2. These should be outfits that you can wear to work on any day. They should look professional, not too formal (like you're going to a wedding) nor too casual (like you're going to a nightclub, a yoga class, or the beach...unless that's your workplace, of course). If you want, you can use the pants of one outfit as the pants of another outfit. Find one or two pairs of shoes that fit with all the outfits. This forms your capsule wardrobe.

4. Place your remaining work clothes (those that aren't part of your capsule wardrobe) in garment bags, boxes, etc., and store these away from your bedroom closet.

5. Place all the elements of each outfit together on the same hanger if possible. Include socks and other accessories needed to

complete the outfit. The idea is to not have to 'pull the outfit together' in the morning.

6. On the morning of Day 1, choose the first outfit in your closet; choose the second outfit on Day 2, and so on.

7. During the weekend, wash clothes as needed, and put your outfits together again, mixing and matching as desired.

8. During the second week, repeat the process (6 then 7).

9. Regularly, for example, at the beginning of a season, evaluate your capsule wardrobe and make changes as desired.

10. Make decisions about the work clothes being stored. Do you want to:
    a. Continue storing them?
    b. Trade them for items that are part of the capsule wardrobe?
    c. Give them away to family, friends, or charity?
    d. Sell them (consignment, Kijiji, eBay)?
    e. Other

11. Don't buy new clothes unless you want to replace an item in your capsule wardrobe. You might want to reduce the temptation to buy new clothes by avoiding shopping centers altogether. Find other forms of entertainment! ☺

4

Reduce Commuting Time

"Sorry I'm late for our meeting, Roxanne," Tim said breathlessly, "Once again, I was stuck in traffic. If it's not an accident, there's construction and zipper merges that no one seems to know how to do. I must spend two hours a day sitting in my car, pounding my fists on the steering wheel, weaving in and out of lanes, beeping my horn, and yelling at stupid drivers. By the time I get to work and, later, back home, I need another hour or more to decompress. I'm just fed up with this hassle."

"Wow, you sound frustrated, Tim. You live about half an hour away from downtown Bridge City, don't you?

"Yes, but the traffic is heavy, so, door-to-door, it takes an hour. I'm beat. How do you do it? Don't you live in the same area, Roxanne?"

"I sure do. I don't know if you noticed it or not, Tim, but I only come to the office four days a week, and I work extra-long hours on those days. Because of that, I'm not traveling during rush hour. So, the trip is reasonably quick and peaceful."

"Lucky you. I didn't know that this flextime arrangement was possible. When was it announced?"

"It wasn't announced. I just asked for it when I was hired. You know, just because there isn't an official policy, it doesn't mean that something can't be done. What's that expression? 'You don't make 100% of the shots that you don't try.' ("Uhh... Wayne Gretsky said that you miss 100% of the shots that you don't take.") Anyhow, I wish that I could simply take the bus or ride my bike. That would be ideal. But because I see clients on those four days, I have to drive my own vehicle. So, I use the driving time to listen to minimalism podcasts and various audiobooks. It's a win-win. I arrive at the office full of energy and ready to work, and later on, when I get home, my family and I sit down to a late dinner and relax."

"You make it sound so easy. For you, it seems that travel is a non-issue. One less hassle. One less worry…"

"If I could live downtown, my commuting time would be zero. But there aren't any schools downtown for my children, and –"

"Oh, zero commuting time would be great, but the cost-of-living downtown is so much higher than where I live right now. And I, too, have a family to consider. Besides, from what I can see, your flextime arrangement seems to be a win-win situation for everyone. Our workplace gets an employee who isn't frazzled and potentially late. You work extra hours when fewer people are around and, thus, are more productive. Your family has you at home for supper, and you're less drained. You enjoy the commute more because you're wasting less time stuck in traffic. And, if more people did this, there would be less congestion on the roads."

"I hope you can see its link with minimalism: it simplifies my schedule and gives me a calmer, more compressed commuting experience, which, in turn, gives me the time needed to do what is more meaningful for me. Some people even work from home one or more days a week. That's not a fit for my job, but it is an option for others. Anyhow, take a look at Tool 4. There are lots of options available."

~ ~ ~

After much reflection and consideration of his options, Tim decided to request a special work arrangement: he would work five days a week, but start and finish his workday an hour earlier than usual. His commutes to and from work outside of rush hour became relaxed and a good opportunity to brush up on his Spanish. He was planning to walk the 800 km Camino pilgrimage across northern Spain in a couple of years. Lo and behold, soon enough, another brick fell off his back. Muy bien!

Tool 4 – Reduce commuting time

"For many people, commuting is the worst part of the day, and policies that can make commuting shorter and more convenient would be a straightforward way to reduce minor but widespread suffering." – Daniel Kahneman

"I had an insanely long commute...I hate to waste time, so I spent my time [on the train] writing about my life on the premise that I might be able to pitch those as short essays to magazines. It wasn't until later that I realized that I was writing a book." – Charles M. Blow

"Improbable as it may be, the day still has a few indignities left. All of them from every floor are crammed into this one subway car: the makers of memos, the routers of memos, the indexers, filers, and shredders of memos, the always-at-their-desks, and the never-around. Squabbling like pigeons over stale crumbs of seats. Everyone thinks they are more deserving, everyone thinks their day has been harder than everyone else's, and everyone is correct." — Colson Whitehead

Get Closer ~ Flextime ~ Work @ Home ~ Use Travel Time ~ Change Your Mode ~ ROWE

- ☑ Live closer to where you work (or the reverse).
- ☑ Commute during off-hours when there's less traffic.
- ☑ Work from home more frequently (or always).
- ☑ Use your commuting time productively.
- ☑ Adopt the most efficient mode of transportation possible.
- ☑ Look into adopting a Results Only Work Environment where results rather than physical presence are rewarded.

Tool 4 – Roxanne's Tips

1. Be clear about what's in it for you to reduce your commuting time. There are opportunity costs to commuting that you need to take into account. If you add up how much time you might spend commuting throughout your career (if you keep doing what you're doing now), you would be flabbergasted by how much it actually costs you in terms of increased frustration and stress, vehicle maintenance and gas, and time that you could have spent with your family, enjoying a hobby, or chillaxing.

2. Live closer to where you work (or vice versa). Is it possible to find a job that is close to where you live, or, more likely, find a place to live that is a reasonable distance from where you work? When assessing distance, consider both your commuting time and mode of transportation. For example, if you live close to a subway station or a direct bus to your workplace, even though the

distance is longer, the commuting time might be shorter. Sometimes living closer to where you work means living downtown or increasing your living costs. If this isn't your thing and if you can't afford to buy a house in a neighborhood close to your work, don't worry. There are other options.

3. Commute during off-hours when there's less traffic. Drive or take the bus/subway when there's less congestion. See if you can extend your hours so that you begin and end working before (or after) rush hour starts. For example, if it takes you an hour to get to work during the 8 am morning rush hour, try leaving at 7 am. It should significantly reduce your travel time. If your workplace doesn't have this kind of policy, go ahead and ask if you can be the 'pilot project.'

4. Commute to work less often. This involves two options:

   a. See if you can work longer hours for 4 days a week instead of going to work 5 days a week. For example, if you normally work 8 hours/day, that adds up to 40 hours per week. Try to fit those 40 hours into 4 days by arriving earlier, taking a shorter lunch, and/or leaving later. Again, go ahead and ask for this 'informal arrangement,' if a formal flextime policy doesn't exist.

   b. Work from home more frequently. Yes, why not have a home office? There'll be less time (and money) wasted commuting (so it's better for the environment), fewer interruptions, and increased productivity. Try this once per week or every two weeks to see how it works. You'll still be available to clients and others via phone, Zoom, or Teams, and email. Tell your boss that you would like to try telecommuting or remote working as a 'pilot project.' A word of caution: if you choose this option, you need to be self-motivated and self-managing. If you need constant prodding and direction from your boss or others, this might be a disaster.

5. Use your commuting time productively. Learn French or listen to audiobooks (borrowed from the library) or minimalism podcasts while you're driving. Read a book, read the newspaper, plan your day, or observe [and possibly chat up others (but be sensible about this)] while you're on the bus. Get some exercise by riding a bike or walking to work (if possible). This may turn out to be your chief source of cardio.

6. Adopt the most efficient mode of transportation possible. Don't always insist on taking your car if it's possible to get to work using public transit (and do some work at the same time) or on foot (biking or walking). Alternatively, consider carpooling with folks from your neighborhood who work downtown. Unfortunately, this option may not be available to those whose jobs require them to visit clients using their personal vehicles.

7. Look into adopting a Results Only Work Environment (ROWE) where results rather than physical presence are rewarded. Although your workplace may not be prepared to introduce a full-fledged ROWE for everyone in all job categories, see if they can introduce a modified version for you. For example, do a pilot project (yes, another one) in which your boss agrees to not monitor how much facetime you put in at work in exchange for your achieving a predefined set of results. The proof will be in your increased productivity and results. If you have proven in the past that you are a productive and self-driven worker who doesn't need constant monitoring, you might be able to convince your boss to give this a try.

5

Avoid Electronic Time Eaters

"Did you get my email, Tim?" Roxanne asked as she stepped into Tim's office.

"Possibly. I'll check," Tim replied as he opened his

email account. With Roxanne at his side, prompting him to search for her name, he was able to find her email. It was buried in an inbox that contained several hundred emails.

"What's going on Tim? Why do you have so many emails in your inbox? For how long have they been in there? And how do you manage to get your work done?"

"Hmm…I don't know. Some have probably been in there for a year or two. I don't really notice these things. I just check my emails as soon as I hear the ping. I scan them quickly and, if I feel like answering them, I do. Otherwise, if I judge them to be super urgent, I usually answer right away. I just leave them in the inbox in case I need to refer to them later."

"So, you check your emails as soon as you receive them throughout the day, regardless of what you're doing at the moment?"

"Yeah, they might be important. I also check them on weekends, evenings, and holidays. I'm always available to the company."

"Wow. Well, first of all, by answering emails throughout the day, including at the very start of the day, you are allowing others' priorities to become your priority. You lose your concentration on whatever you're working on. Isn't what you're doing important? If there is a real emergency, someone will call you. And, second, by never taking a break from emails, you're always on-call – you're tethered to your job. You need to set some boundaries or else you'll never be fully 'present' for your family or whatever else you're doing."

"I know. I have ruined a vacation or two by checking out my work emails rather than just relaxing. And now that you mention it, sometimes, when the end of the day arrives, I find that I've been emailing all day and evening. I've frittered away my time. I vow to do better, but the cycle continues. And despite all this, I still don't seem to make any inroads in the overall volume of emails I receive."

"Have you subscribed to a lot of newsletters and promotional emails? You could probably unsubscribe from a bunch of them or, at the very least, have all of these emails directed to a folder labeled 'Reading' or something like that."

"That would be a good first step; it would stem the tide of future informational emails. But what should I do with all the emails that are currently in my inbox? I just don't have the time or energy to deal with them. They may be important. I can't just delete them, can I?"

"Hmm…some people might tell you to delete them all, since people may re-send any vital emails. However, I'm a bit more cautious. In your shoes, I wouldn't delete them. Some emails may contain information that you'll need to refer back to in the future. Ideally, you would take an hour or more and go through all of them, or at least those that seem important. If this isn't possible, I have something radical to suggest."

"Yes?"

"Move them all to a folder labeled 'Old Inbox' or something like that and wipe the slate clean. You'll have an empty inbox for a fresh start."

"That would be a great stress reliever, Roxanne. But won't my inbox just fill up again?"

"Yes, Tim. If you keep doing what you've always done, you'll continue to have the same results you've always had. So, you may want to change when you access your emails and what you do once you access them."

"There's that word again – change!"

"Tool 5 suggests that you consult your emails in chunks or blocks of time that start only after you have worked on your priorities. During these blocks, for each email, you need to determine if you can provide an on-the-spot response within approximately 5 minutes. If it's possible, go ahead and respond. If you need to forward the email to someone else for their assistance, do this now. The idea is to read each email only once and deal with it immediately. Then, for emails that require you to do more work, note what you have to do on your to-do list, schedule when you'll do it, and move on. Your inbox becomes an 'outstanding items' folder that you empty when you have dealt with the items. Then, you can file the emails in folders that match the ones that you have on your computer. Productivity expert Merlin Mann, who came up with the idea of Zero Inbox, calls this the 'Delete, Delegate, Respond, Defer or Do' principle."

"Hmm, it sounds like I need to be more disciplined than I currently am. I kind of like checking emails right away ("Not mine though, eh?"). It's a break from work. And I guess I'm a bit scatterbrained, but I flit from one email to another without dealing with them, often reading them several times. I can see how your approach can save me time and help me concentrate on my work. I'll try it! What have I got to lose?"

"Now, about your cellphone –"

"Don't worry. I do try to turn off notifications, and I keep it on vibrate when I'm doing important stuff. Also, when I'm meeting with someone, I let my calls go to voicemail."

"That's a good start, Tim, but it might not be enough. Some researchers found that the 'mere presence of your phone reduces your cognitive capacity.'"

"What?????"

"Yup. In an experiment, Kristen Duke and her buddies gave people a task to do, and the best results and concentration came from people whose phones were in another room. Next were people whose phones were in their pockets. People who kept their phones on their desks had the worst performance. In fact, their performance was similar to that of folks who were sleep-deprived. They had low focus, creativity, and effectiveness. According to these researchers, 'the mere presence of our smartphones is like the sound of our names – they are constantly calling to us, exerting a gravitational pull on our attention.'"

"Sadly, I agree. I feel drawn to check my phone all the time! What should I do?"

"Kristen Duke and her buddies recommend that you define a period of time when you won't be consulting your phone and, furthermore, that you ask employees to not bring their phones to meetings."

"Oh, that's a big ask, but it might make for an interesting pilot project. We could try it and see how it impacts our productivity. If our meetings become shorter and more focused, then people might agree to it. Hmm…there are lots of other electronic time eaters and distractors, you know: the Internet, YouTube, texting, social media, games, you name it. Why aren't you offering tips on these?"

"Ah… yes, I do realize that there are employees who access all of that while at work. But I'm concentrating on what I consider to be the two biggest electronic time wasters: email and smartphones. And most people know they shouldn't be accessing those sites for personal reasons while at work. It's a form of time theft."

"Yikes! When you put it that way, I'll think twice about posting a picture of me at the coffee shop on Facebook during work hours."

"You might find Shaun Achor's recommendation useful. He says that we should make positive habits '20 seconds' easier to start and negative habits '20 seconds' harder to start. So, for example, as a way of reducing the temptation to look at your emails, you could sign out of your email program as soon as you're done looking at your emails. The delay and hassle involved in signing back in might be enough to discourage you from casually accessing your emails and other sites."

"That might just work! And it's so tempting to check my emails at night. I keep thinking that something urgent might come up.

But, in all honesty, there is rarely anything that can't wait till the next morning. Okay, I will make a concerted effort to not check my emails during family dinners and my leisure activities."

~ ~ ~

With that, Roxanne returned to her office, and Tim contemplated his next step. Moving all the inbox emails to a separate folder gave him an immediate sense of relief. Whew! 'Now, I can start fresh,' he said to himself. The most difficult part was training himself not to constantly access his emails. However, over (lots of) time and after re-reading the Tool sheets and giving in to temptation and re-beginning, Tim learned to tame electronic clutter. One day, while he was focused on his priorities without even thinking about the emails that awaited him, a brick quietly slid off Tim's back.

Tool 5 – Avoid Electronic Time Eaters

"No one ever got rich checking their email more often." – Noah Kagan

"Turn off your email; turn off your phone; disconnect from the Internet; figure out a way to set limits so you can concentrate when you need to and disengage when you need to." – Gretchen Rubin

"It's not the sheer number and volume of distractions that gets us into trouble; it's the ease of access to them." – Shaun Achor

Priorities ~ Blocks ~ Empty inbox ~ Brief/Polite ~ Disconnect

- ☑ Start your day with <u>your</u> priorities.
- ☑ Consult emails in blocks of time.
- ☑ Respond to emails requiring 5 minutes or less as soon as you open them.
- ☑ Keep an empty or nearly empty inbox.
- ☑ Be brief <u>and</u> polite.
- ☑ Sign out from social media, email programs, and anything else that takes your attention away from your work.

Tool 5 – Roxanne's Tips

1. Figure out <u>why</u> you want to manage your electronic time eaters. What's in it for you? As work-life balance researcher Marcello Russo and his buddies discovered, identifying why you want to manage your use of technology more effectively is essential. They identify several motivations, such as improving performance, crafting a personal digital philosophy about the role that technology should play in your life, or reducing inappropriate behaviors in social settings.

2. Stay focused on your priorities. Start your day by looking at your agenda and your list of things to accomplish for the day. THOSE are your priorities, not your emails or your cell phone. Don't start your day with someone else's priorities.

3. Consult emails in blocks of time. Set aside several blocks of time throughout the day to read and process your emails in batches of, say, 30 minutes. Merlin Mann suggests processing your emails on the hour (for example, 11 am) throughout the day. To remove distractions, remove any notifications indicating that you have received an email. Except for these email periods, keep your email program closed so that you're not tempted to check your emails. In other words, make it a hassle to access your email: log off every time you finish using your email or connect to your email only via a web browser (rather than using a shortcut or a phone app).

4. Read an email only once. When you read an email, act on it. Don't just read it and ignore it. This guarantees that you'll have to read it a second time.

    i. Respond immediately to emails that require 5 minutes or less to handle. This includes forwarding emails to others as needed.
    ii. Add important tasks (arising from emails that take more than 5 minutes) to a to-do list and/or your calendar.
    iii. Either file the rest in subfolders that match those on your computer or delete them.

5. Keep an empty (or nearly empty) inbox. If you have hundreds of emails in your inbox, 'clear the deck' and move them to an archive subfolder. This allows you to start fresh.

6. Be brief but be polite:
    a. Get to the point quickly and nicely in your emails. Long emails place demands on other people's time, not to mention yours!
    b. Watch your tone. Be respectful: avoid aggressiveness or bossiness. Emails that are too direct come across as rude.
    c. Don't send an email when you're angry or frustrated. You might regret it! Sleep on it overnight if possible.
    d. Don't 'reply all' and cc the whole office on your emails. Ask yourself who really needs to know what you're communicating.
    e. Don't write in an email what you wouldn't want to see in your boss's hands or on the front page of the newspaper, for example:
        i. Letting your coworkers know that you think that your boss is a fool/hot/on their way out.
        ii. Telling a buddy about your drunken escapade last night.
        iii. Sharing sexist cartoons and jokes with your coworkers.
        iv. Inviting your lover to come to your place tonight and...
        v. Trying to sell some random personal items, such as used tires, to your coworkers.

6

Focus on the Vital Few

"Hey Roxanne!" Tim said as he poked his head into her office, "I've got it made now. Five fewer bricks. Less stuff. No decisions to make first thing in the morning. Easier commute. Clean inbox. I'm good."

"Hey Tim!" Roxanne replied, "That's good to hear. I'm glad the tools are working for you."

"This minimalism stuff is pretty easy, after all," Tim said, "I've got it covered."

"Whoa there, Tim. Dealing with stuff is the easy part. Getting rid of the physical clutter, cutting your commute, and clearing your inbox is like picking off the low-hanging fruit: they're the easiest part of the process. ("Groan!") The rest of the fruit – the more foundational elements – are on higher branches and require lots of stretching. These fruits deal with YOU – looking at how and why you do stuff, your mental clutter, people clutter, and all the rest of the stuff. Of course, you can just go on your merry way and be proud of what you've accomplished so far. But you still have lots of bricks on your back. Want to get rid of them too?"

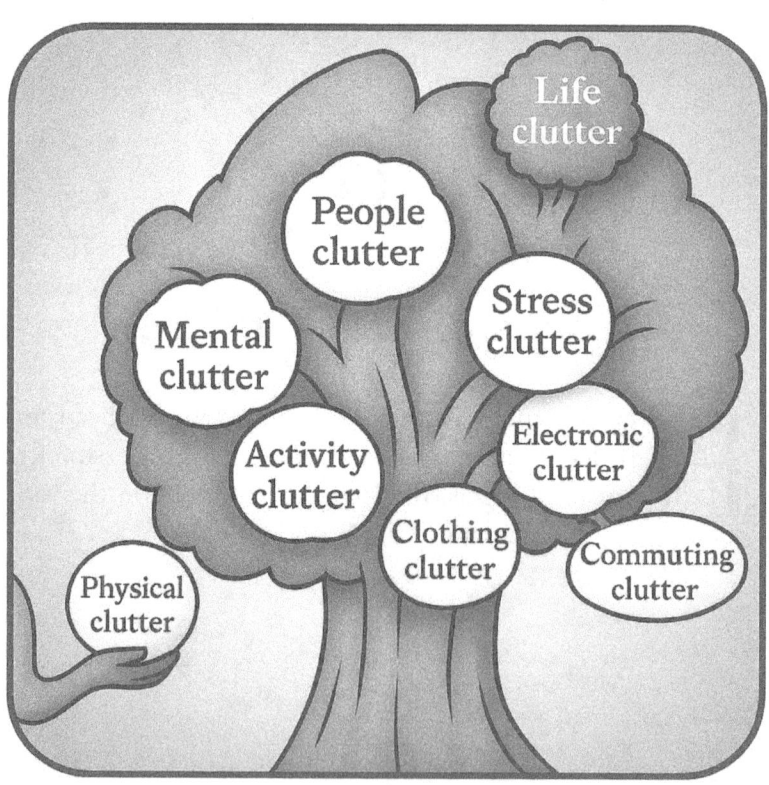

"Just when I thought I was done! Yes, of course, I want to get rid of them, but this stuff sounds deep and like a lot of work."

"It's your choice. I think you've liked your results so far."

"Well, you're right, but what's the next tool?"

"The next tool gets you to look at how you're doing your work and figure out the most effective way of doing it. This means starting with your major goals and —"

"Oh, I've got goals up my yin-yang. There's nothing new and exciting about this. I just can't get everything done. I'm being stretched everywhere, fighting fires, managing crises, burning the midnight oil. You know…"

"I used to 'know,' Tim, but I realized that, despite my busyness, I really wasn't getting much accomplished in terms of my major goals. I was trying to be everything to everyone, and, sure, I was working hard, but at what cost? My work time flowed into my home time because it was easier to let things slide a bit and then a bit more and a bit more till it became my way of doing things, and it was expected of me. I figured that if I didn't get everything done by quitting time, well, I just wouldn't quit. And, as you know, with our kind of work, there's always something to do."

> **Shun perfectionism.** That extra time spent fussing over minor details is better invested in your vital few. 'Well done' beats 'never finished.'

"Don't I know it!"

"Well, I think that a good place to start is the Vital Few Exercise. You know the classic Pareto Principle? ("Yeah…"). Well, in his book called *The 4-Hour Workweek*, Tim Ferriss talks about how you can use this principle to get rid of 50% of your workload by investing your time in the 20% of things that get you 80% of your results."

"Oh, I heard about that book. Doesn't he also try to outsource tasks in his personal and work life to virtual assistants in other countries for really cheap? I imagine that this frees him up to do what he wants."

"Yes, he does talk about that. His main point, however, is what I'm saying here: we need to focus on the vital few. You can begin by writing down your list of tasks – absolutely all of them – leaving room on the page for two small columns. For each task, rate its importance from 1 (trivial) to 10 (vital) and how time-intensive it is from 1 (takes very little time) to 10 (time-intensive). Then, analyze what you've written. If you're spending lots of time on something trivial, that's a red flag: your priorities are screwed up, and you need to rethink how you're investing your time. Verify whether you're spending most of your time on these. If not, figure out why. If something is relatively trivial, you should be spending little or no time on it. Maybe it's something that you can delegate or stop doing entirely. This is important. Your focus should be on what's vital and central to your work."

"Okay, so the idea is to stop burying myself in the trivial many and focus on the vital few. Unfortunately, by the time I finish doing all the trivial stuff, half my day is already over, and I just don't have the energy to work on the bigger projects."

> **IT CAN TAKE A LOT MORE TIME AND ENERGY TO PROCRASTINATE THAN TO DO THE WORK THAT YOU'RE AVOIDING. GET STARTED AND THE MOTIVATION WILL COME.**

"I used to do this, too. There's a sense of accomplishment that comes with getting the trivial stuff out of the way, and it's (usually) easy, mindless stuff. I had to work hard to train myself to devote my mornings to the vital few (because my energy level is highest in the morning). So, I never schedule meetings in the morning. That way, the trivial stuff gets my 'leftover' time and energy, and not the reverse. As management consultant Brian Tracy argues, we must 'eat that frog!' He says that a frog is our biggest priority, and not only do we have to get to it first, but we have to eat the ugliest one first. ("Yuk!") Apparently, he was quoting Mark Twain, who said, 'Eat a live frog first thing in the morning and nothing worse will happen to you the rest of the day.'"

"Hmm...So, this is about good time and energy management, in part. Focus, focus, focus seems to be the key. I have to stop frittering away my time and having nothing to show for my day at the end of the day. You know, I have trouble saying 'no' when someone comes by my office and wants to chat or asks a question. As of yesterday, I have a new project that one of our colleagues handed to me that is really his responsibility."

"This kind of reverse delegation – handing off tasks to others that belong to you – is common. Have you heard the expression 'get the monkey off your back'? ("No...") Well, the monkey represents someone else's responsibility or burden that they are shifting onto you."

"Hey, I've got enough bricks to carry without having to do someone else's monkey too!"

"We're carrying other people's monkeys when we agree to do things that they should be doing themselves. All the little things add up. You have to develop a spine and be willing to say 'no' or – at the very least – establish boundaries. Say what you're willing to do and be clear about your role. You might want to coach that colleague on how to do the project. Otherwise, you become an easy target – an overloaded one at that."

"Oh, I get it. Our co-worker Joe keeps sending me his sales reports and asking me to review them for errors and omissions. He makes such careless mistakes; he doesn't even check his spelling. I've been investing lots of time in doing this, and I mean LOTS of time. He loves my work! But what you're saying is that this is his bailiwick, not mine, and I have to draw the line so that his work doesn't become mine. Maybe I've been fostering his dependence on me. He may be careless in preparing his reports because he knows that I will correct his errors and oversights. From what I can see, my choices are to say 'no' outright, suggest that we meet and go through his report together (so that I can show him how to correct it himself and so that he's using some of his own time for this), or say that I have only 10 minutes available instead of the two hours that I've been investing…"

"That's a good example and good options. Be prepared for some pushback on his part. He'll be cranky because you're changing the 'terms of your implicit agreement,' you know, how things have always been done, but he'll get used to it if you stay firm. By the way, when I first started here, Joe told me to check his reports for him, but I didn't comply. Resistance is not futile!"

"Great Star Trek reference… Anyhow, I'll go through the tool and try to get a better handle on my work instead of wasting time on tasks that don't make a difference and doing other people's work. Thanks, Roxanne, for the timely tips."

~ ~ ~

With that, Tim strolled into his office, took out a pad of paper, and did the Vital Few Exercise. He then circled his three most vital tasks. For each of these tasks, he identified the deliverables (the milestones and results that are expected) and the next steps. He thought about how he could do his work more efficiently, and he found a couple of shortcuts. Then, in his "time planner," he wrote the three tasks that he must do the next day to achieve the deliverables and the order in which he will do them. He blocked off two hours of uninterrupted time during his high-energy period (first thing in the morning) to focus on the tasks.

The next morning, he told his boss and his secretary that he would be unavailable for a couple of hours while he focused on a critical work project. He put a "Do not disturb" sign on his door, his cellphone on airplane mode (and in his drawer), and he got to work. After two hours, he marveled at his achievements: focusing on one task at a time without distractions (self-generated or otherwise) significantly boosted his productivity. The tasks took less time than usual to complete because Tim was able to develop a sense of flow and focus by concentrating on his work.

At noon, Tim went for a walk and chatted with his colleagues without feeling guilty about the work that was undone. When coworkers 'offered' projects to him, he considered how they fit with his vital few and how time-intensive they might be. If they were vital and if he had the time to do them, he would accept them, but only with clearly defined roles and responsibilities. He would assist, but never take ownership of someone else's project.

At the end of every day, he would plan for the following day. Sure, there were occasional, unexpected demands on his time, but he just went with the flow and doubled his efforts to focus on his vital few. Because of his efforts, Tim felt better able to focus on his work. And after continuing this process for a month, it became a habit, and a brick slid off his back.

Tool 6 – Focus on the vital few

"It is about making the wisest possible investment of your time and energy in order to operate at your highest point of contribution by doing only what is essential." –Greg McKeown

"Doing something unimportant well does not make it important." –Timothy Ferriss

Quality consultant Joseph Juran created the law of the vital few, also known as the Pareto principle. According to this law, 80% of results come from 20% of your efforts. The 20% is vital, and the rest of your efforts are trivial. The trivial many will always exist. Too many people spend too much time doing stuff that means too little. When you waste your time, you waste your life. And work expands to fill the time available: if you have two hours to write a report, it will take you two hours. If you have one hour, it will take you one hour. Bottom line: you need to focus your resources, time, and talents on the vital few things that really matter and make a difference.

Vital Few ~ Focus ~ Efficient ~ Routine

- ☑ Determine the Big 3: three vital things to accomplish today.
- ☑ Assign time blocks for these vital things in your calendar.
- ☑ Manage your energy.
- ☑ Focus on efficiently accomplishing vital things.
- ☑ Say no to reverse delegation.

- ☑ Use the resources around you.
- ☑ Develop a routine that works for you.

Tool 6 – Roxanne's Tips

1. Figure out the most important results or deliverables that you need to achieve and what you must do to achieve those results. Based on this list, identify the Big 3: the three most vital things that you will do 'the next day' that will directly impact your achieving these results. If you get these things done, at the end of the day, you should feel like you've had a super productive day. Decide the order in which you will do The Big 3.

2. Reserve blocks of time in your daily calendar to do The Big 3. These should be periods when you're at your highest energy level and when your time is least likely to be in demand by others. If these two blocks clash, then find a creative way to compromise. Unless something changes your priorities or is extraordinarily urgent, keep your promise to yourself.

3. Manage your energy! Keep tabs on your energy levels throughout the day. Be sure to give yourself a mini break away from your office regularly so that you can boost your energy levels. According to Tony Schwartz and Catherine McCarthy, both from The Energy Project, even a few minutes of disengaging from work boosts your energy levels and helps you maintain positive emotions. They offer the example of Matthew Lang, managing director of Sony in South Africa, who found that his 20-minute afternoon walks increased his creativity.

4. Focus on your work. Don't simply react to potential distractions. Distractions and interruptions will always beckon our attention.

Resist them! Focus on what's most important. Consider what typically distracts you (such as drop-in visitors or miscellaneous tasks) and make a plan to minimize those distractions. For example, sign out of your email account, put your cell phone on airplane mode, ask your secretary (if you have one) to hold your calls for a block of time, close your door, and have all the needed resources at hand. While you're at it, figure out what else steals your time from your important work and deal with it.

5. Don't multitask. It means that none of your work is getting your full attention. It hinders your productivity, and getting back on task is time-consuming! Research by Stanford researcher Eyal Ophir and his buddies shows that multitasking only leads to people spreading themselves thin, feeling stressed, and not doing a good job on anything.

6. Reconsider how you're getting your work done:
    a) How can you do your work more simply or efficiently?
    b) What shortcuts can you take that won't affect the quality of your work?
    c) What steps or entire tasks can you eliminate?
    d) Who can take over some of your tasks?
    e) How can you streamline your workflow and work processes?
    f) How can you avoid being reactive to crises and others' demands on your time and, instead, concentrate on your big, longer-term priorities? You may have developed a routine that is comfortable but not optimal.

7. Minimize the number of meetings that you attend. If your participation is essential, work towards getting maximum gain out of a shorter period (have a focused agenda and stick to it). Try walking, standing, or holding electronic meetings. Electronic

meetings (for example, Zoom or Teams) save the time it takes to travel to meetings.

8. Don't let others download their work onto you. Learn to say 'no' nicely when asked to do work that others should be doing themselves. There are plenty of opportunities to get involved in others' projects, provide assistance, and engage in random tasks. Unless you say no (or at least, "not now") to downloaders, they will keep knocking at your door. You can do a colleague a favor every once in a while, but only after your vital three have been done that day.

9. Deal with interruptions before they eat up your time. First, keep track of them: when they happen, who's interrupting your work, and what the topic is. Then, especially for top interrupters, consider using the tactics recommended by professional organizer Stephanie Culp:
    a) Start work early when no one's around the office,
    b) Keep your office door closed,
    c) Stand up and start walking out when folks arrive at your door (ask if they would like to 'walk and talk'), or
    d) Ask 'How can I help you?' as a way of focusing the conversation.

    Also, be mindful of how often you may be interrupting others' work!

7

Eliminate Mental Clutter

"**I'm baaaack!**" Tim said as he plopped into Roxanne's guest chair while clutching the Tool 7 pages. "Thanks for agreeing to meet with me. I'm having trouble seeing how my way of thinking relates to minimalism. Please enlighten me."

"Sure, Tim," Roxanne said, "Remember the first sheets that described what minimalism is?"

"Yessss…" Tim replied hesitantly.

"Well, the goal of minimalism is to purge life's excess (such as a glut of distractions, commitments, and complexities in our lives) and focus on what's most important (by getting rid and letting go of stuff that isn't important), so that you find meaning, peace, and freedom in your life. ("Sounds good so far…") It's not enough to simply deal with physical clutter. We all have mental clutter too; for example: being easily distracted by the glut of information and possibilities and demands on our time, overcommitting, or being too attached to ego, recognition, and status (which create their own problems)."

"Well, getting rid of the physical clutter has already helped me organize my thoughts and be less distracted. Based on what you're saying, I have to take a good look at what's cluttering my mind, figure out what I want to keep, and let go of the rest. Right?"

"Yes, essentially that's it. So much of what holds us back from peace, meaning, and freedom is our own doing – our own thoughts and emotions. Eliminating mental clutter means focusing on what's most important in the present moment, taking charge of your own destiny through self-discipline, eliminating thinking errors that distort your perception of the world, and taking responsibility for yourself. There's lots more that you can do, of course, but I found that these were the essentials for me."

"So, simplicity and clear thinking are key."

"Yes, I really like what André Klein has to say about it. He says that we need to take our 'minds to the dumpster' by seriously culling the amount of information that we expose ourselves to and 'dis-identifying from mental manure (you may have lots of stuff in your mind, but that's not necessarily who you are).'"

"Oh….mental manure. Sounds like a dirty job."

"It can be. The first thing I did was to pay attention to my thinking processes. In fact, in 15-minute increments for an entire day, I wrote down everything that came to mind: the topics and examples. ("Oh man, that's time-consuming…") Yes, the time investment was heavy, but it was worth it. At the end of the day, I was able to evaluate:

→ How focused I was on the task at hand. Was I fully concentrating on the task, or did I willingly allow my thoughts to drift to something else? Was I easily distracted by too much information?

→ Whether my thoughts were primarily in the present, past, or future. Was worry my constant companion?

→ Whether I was managing myself by being proactive (instead of reactive), delaying gratification (instead of responding immediately to my moment-to-moment wants), tolerating frustration (instead of blowing up), and thinking before speaking or doing (instead of being impulsive). This was an eye-opener.

→ How often I put a negative spin on things. Was I distorting reality to fit my expectations? I easily slid into this dark mess.

→ How often I felt like I was at the mercy of others and simply a victim of circumstances. More often than I expected, as it turns out!"

"Oh wow, that's intense…" Roger murmured.

"You can bet that I developed a good picture of how much mental clutter I was storing in the attic of my mind. Knowing all of this motivated me to do something about it. ("Time to take out the garbage!") I consciously tried to:

a) **Live in the present moment**; that is, be fully conscious of my senses (hearing, sight, smell, taste, and touch) and feelings,

b) **Face and challenge my perceptual errors and cognitive distortions**, and

c) **Recalibrate my attention** by breathing deeply and focusing on the present moment.

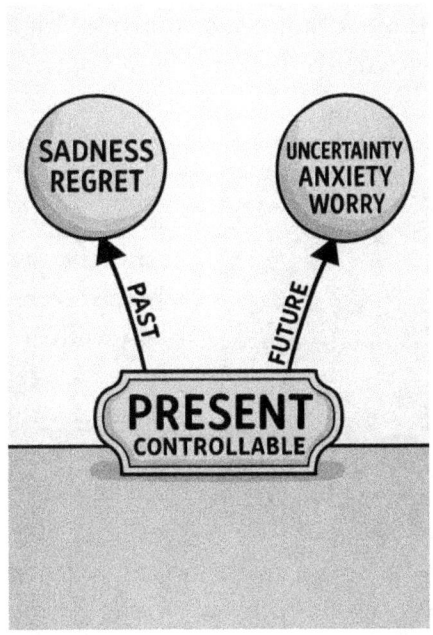

Also, I found that a walk through the park next to our office helped me feel more grounded. It wasn't easy, and I slid back into my old ways ~~at times~~ often, but over time, I managed to clear out some of the clutter. Bit by bit. It's a work in progress."

"Hmm… if I were to evaluate my thinking processes, I might need to order a dumpster to haul away the junk that's littering my mind."

"Good luck with that, Tim. I think it all boils down to mindset. According to Stanford psychologist Carol Dweck, people have either fixed or growth mindsets. If you have a fixed mindset, you believe that there's not much you can change about your basic traits and that 'talent alone creates success – without effort.' Your internal dialogue is focused on judging yourself, others, and all that you perceive. You give up easily on yourself and others. In contrast, people with a growth mindset consider traits and talents to be flexible; they can develop them, learn, and change. Their internal dialogue is focused not on judging, but on learning and improving and helping others do the same."

"So, we CAN change and improve! Yikes, there's lots to do. How will I know when I'm done with Tool 7 and can move on to Tool 8?"

"Good question. I'm still using Tool 7, and I think I'll be using it for the rest of my life. You know the 'whack a mole' game where moles pop out, and you hit them with a hammer for points? ("Ya...") Well, I think of mental clutter as those moles and the Tool as the hammer. The key to whacking the moles is to realize that they exist in the first place. And once you do this, you might notice that there are tons of moles, and you can't keep up with the whacking. It might be so exhausting that you're tempted to give up. After a while, however, once you've been eliminating the mental clutter, you'll see fewer and fewer moles pop up. When it becomes manageable, then you can probably move on to Tool 8.

"Thanks, Roxanne. I'll keep this in mind....literally."

~ ~ ~

And with that, Tim shuffled back to his office and re-read the tool sheets. Tim decided to read the tool sheets first thing in the morning every day for as long as it took to clean out his mind's attic. At the end of each day, he would place a checkmark beside the tips he used and an "x" beside those he botched. He told himself that he wouldn't move on to Tool 8 till he had a day (mostly) full of checkmarks. It was a challenge for Tim to let go of his habitual – and automatic – pessimism and sense of helplessness. But he knew that these weren't working for him, so he persisted in his efforts to rid himself of his mental clutter.

Finally, for a brief moment one day, Tim experienced a sense of calm. He wasn't easily rattled, angered, or distracted. And a couple of bricks slipped off his back. Unfortunately, they landed in a wheelbarrow that he was hauling behind himself (unknowingly). Oops! The calm was illusory: Tim had more work to do to ensure that real change happened. Tim worked hard to make the changes permanent. He consciously applied Tool 7 till it became something that he naturally did. And the bricks fell out of the wheelbarrow and disintegrated.

Tool 7 – Eliminate Mental Clutter

"The skillful management of attention is the sine qua non of the good life and the key to improving virtually every aspect of your experience, from mood to productivity to relationships...what you focus on from this moment will create the life and person yet to be." –Winifred Gallagher

"What if we decided to declutter thoughts that no longer (or never) served us? What if we agreed not to add anything to our plates until something is removed? What if we achieved 'inbox zero' for our brains?!?" – Paul Jarvis

"The difference between great people and everyone else is that great people create their lives actively, while everyone else is created by their lives, passively waiting to see where life takes them next. The difference between the two is the difference between living fully and just existing." – Michael Gerber

"Happiness and freedom begin with a clear understanding of one principle: Some things are within our control, and some things are not." – Epictetus

"What is a good person? The one who achieves tranquility by having formed the habit of asking on every occasion, 'What is the right thing to do now?'" – Epictetus

"The biggest obstacle to solving our problems is that we frequently confuse reality with what we make up." – Miles Sherts

"Don't attribute to malice that which can be explained otherwise."
– Alain de Botton

"What disturbs men's minds isn't events but their judgments of events." – Epictetus

"You see what you are willing to see." – John Maxwell

"What happens isn't as important as how you react to what happens." – Thaddeus Golas

"If you change the way you look at things, the things you look at change ... How people treat you is their karma; how you react is yours." – Wayne Dyer

Focus ~ Present ~ Discipline ~ Thinking ~ Ownership

- ☑ Focus on what's in front of you.
- ☑ Live in the present.
- ☑ Engage in self-discipline.
- ☑ Clean up your stinking thinking.
- ☑ Don't play the blame game.

Tool 7 – Roxanne's Tips

1. Focus on what's in front of you. Simplify your way of thinking about things. Clear your mind of distractions, information overload, and 'everything else.' When you allow distractions to pull your attention away from your current priority, you are delegating control to these distractions, and you become unfocused, unproductive, and, yes, unhappy. Ask yourself, "What is the most important thing that I can do/think at this moment?" and then do/think it, focus on it, and don't get pulled into the hazy abyss of 'nothing to show for your time.' According to mindfulness specialist Jon Kabat-Zinn, try to capture the moment! How often do we perform a task while thinking about another obligation, deadline, or what's next in our day? Too often, Kabat-Zinn believes. He suggests that a good way to stay in the present moment is to look at what you're doing and what surrounds you. Observing where our mind is wandering at this moment could tell us whether we are in the present or lost in our thoughts.

2. Live in the present moment. While #1 was about maintaining cognitive control, this point is about attentional control. Unless you have a time machine, you can't change the past, and the only way that you can influence the future is by living in the present. If you tend to talk excessively about your previous successes, experiences, and failures, or if you talk only about your future ambitions, you may be disconnected from the present moment. You should try to distill lessons from the past, but then you need to move on

and apply those lessons to your actions today. When you're depressed about the past or using the past as an excuse for being in a rut, you miss the present moment. When you worry about what might happen in the future, you lose sight of what you can do to influence it now.

3. The key to living in the present moment (and avoiding getting stuck in the past or the future) is mindfulness. Living in the present moment allows us to be more centered, grounded, and in control. According to mindfulness specialist Jon Kabat-Zinn, being mindful is consciously directing one's attention in the present moment and noticing but not judging or analyzing thoughts or sounds that may enter our minds. Mindfulness can help us live instead of getting lost in 'what if' thoughts. It can help us focus less on ulterior motives, live more simply, and let go of distractions and frustration. To practice mindfulness, hit the pause button, and use the small, good moments in your day as encouragement and protection against the stresses of a hectic life. Allow these moments to bring your focus back to what matters in life.

4. Engage in self-discipline. Being able to manage yourself in the immediate future to achieve desired results later is incredibly important. Delayed gratification is at the heart of your ability to work toward achieving goals. Determine the most important things that are likely to distract you and how you plan to reduce their impact. Focus on accomplishing your priorities and goals. Avoid distractions and doing things that divert your attention from your priorities and goals (a familiar tune!). <u>All</u> of your actions have an impact on your future successes, so choose those that allow you to remain motivated and get closer to your goals. You need to maintain your focus on your goals, overcome obstacles, and not be

discouraged. This may sound easy enough, but it isn't. Here are some key elements of self-discipline:

a) Work through challenging situations by not being reactive, but rather, by managing what you say to yourself (and others) and taking positive, constructive actions, even if 'baby steps' are all you can manage at the moment.

b) Delay gratification by holding off on doing things that you feel like doing right now in exchange for bigger rewards later on, in other words, trade short-term and short-lived satisfaction for the achievement of longer-term goals. (For an interesting experiment on this topic, check out Walter Mischel's marshmallow experiment on YouTube.)

c) Tolerate frustration by persevering in the face of competing demands. Someone who slams on his horn and screams insults at other drivers in a traffic jam doesn't tolerate frustration well. Someone who reacts immediately to bad news rather than taking some time to reflect on it is not tolerating frustration well either. ☺

d) Think before speaking or acting. People who think before speaking are less likely to regret what they say or do. Ask yourself if your comments are essential or if you can keep them to yourself. You may need to take a deep breath and count to 10 (or 100) or ask others to give you some time to think about things.

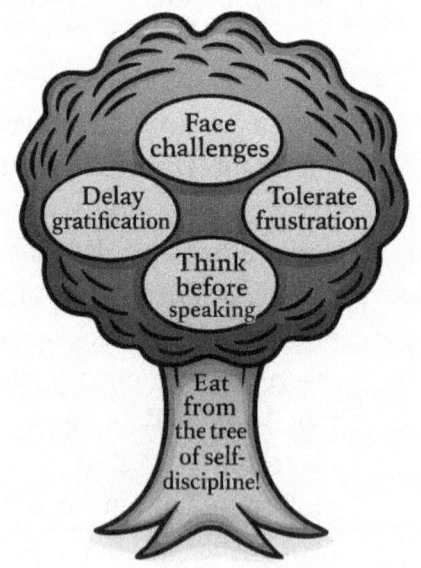

5. Be aware of your stinking thinking. Have you ever been in a situation in which your perception or thoughts about the situation or another person weren't warranted? When you realized that you "jumped the gun"? Usually, this means that perceptual errors and cognitive distortions have seeped into how you see and interpret things. Because a flood of information bombards us, our brains take shortcuts and pay attention to only some of that information. Although this speeds up how we process the world around us, it also results in errors. Combine these perceptual errors with cognitive distortions, which are irrational thought patterns that interfere with how we perceive the world around us (according to psychologist David Burns), and we have a recipe for disaster. Both boil down to not taking the time to think something through and do a reality check. Here are eight common perceptual errors and cognitive distortions:

   a) First impressions: Forming an idea about a person or situation based on our first impression, and then only paying attention to subsequent information that confirms our first impression. For example, if you think that your new co-worker 'Joe' has a great sense of humor when you meet him, as you get to know him, you'll especially notice his sense of humor.

   b) Selective perception or mental filter: Paying attention only to the elements that confirm our existing opinions. For example, if you have a poor opinion of your co-worker, Joe, you will only notice what confirms your perception and ignore any of Joe's strengths. When Roxanne does positive mental filtering concerning her job, she ignores all the negative aspects of the job. When she's doing negative mental filtering, all she sees are the bad things about her job.

c) Halo/horns effect or labeling: Allowing a single characteristic of a person to influence our overall opinion of that person. For example, Tim might think that Roxanne is an overall awesome employee just because she says hello to him as she walks by his office in the morning. As an example of the horns effect, Tim may think that his boss is a tyrant if his boss happens to scold him once for using his cell phone during a meeting.
   d) Projection: Transferring our feelings and preoccupations to another person. For example, Tim might tell others that they look worried when, in reality, it is Tim who is worried.
   e) Stereotyping or clichés: Reducing our perceptions of a situation or a person to categories conveyed in society. For example, Tim may think that Roxanne drives poorly because she's a woman or that Roxanne is 'cultured' because her family is from France.
   f) All-or-nothing thinking: Thinking in extremes: things are either black or white; there aren't any shades of grey. For example, Tim expected to achieve 100% of his sales target, but he achieved only 90% of it, and he feels like a total failure.
   g) Generalization: Making broad claims based on a few examples. For example, thinking that certain things always happen to you or that other things never happen to you, based on a few experiences. For example, Joe missed the bus this morning and concluded that this <u>always</u> happens to him. Or, Joe saw Tim bringing work home one day and concluded that Tim always brings work home. In the same way, people can be prone to exaggeration and minimization. For example, Tim might overestimate the impact of his weaknesses (thinking that they will prevent him from having any kind of career) and, at the same time, minimize the importance of his many talents.

h) Jumping to hasty conclusions or making undue interpretations: Drawing conclusions without taking the time to verify our interpretation and collect more facts. For example, Joe thinks that Tim hates him because Tim pressed the 'close door' button of the elevator just as he was arriving (in reality, Tim meant to press the 'open door' button but got mixed up).

6. Clean up your stinking thinking. Because these errors and biases color your interpretation of the world around you, they create some hefty mental clutter. Here's how to avoid them:
   a) Become aware of them. Don't function on autopilot, unaware of your biases and errors. Stop to think about what you're doing and ask others for their perceptions.
   b) Obtain concrete and objective facts about the situation. Separate the facts from your interpretations, which may be laced with errors and biases. Describe the situation that triggered your error or distortion. In doing so, you will be obliged to relate facts, not your interpretation of these facts. Ask yourself what evidence would be needed to support your point of view, and try to see if this evidence exists. Perhaps, you will see that the situation is not negative after all, or that you overreacted. Don't rush to conclusions; take your time.
   c) Try to see the situation from a variety of perspectives. Put yourself in the other person's shoes and try to understand the situation from their point of view, but also get feedback from others. Leave room for alternative explanations. Give people the benefit of the doubt. Don't presume that they're out to get you. Pay attention to any of your behaviors that might influence the behavior of others. For example, Joe is being aloof toward Tim because he feels that Tim is ignoring him. Now, Tim is

reserved toward Joe because he doesn't understand why Joe's behavior has changed. Joe should realize that Tim's behavior toward him is influenced by his own behavior toward him.

d) Pay attention to any factors or contexts that might influence the situation and that may be beyond everyone's control. The number of errors and distortions that we make increases significantly when situations are unexpected, complex, or unclear, and when we're not sure how to deal with them. Eliminate other potential explanations before blaming the situation on others.

e) Avoid making arbitrary and categorical judgments. Leave room for alternative explanations. Often, by saying what you think out loud, you will find that it is far-fetched or incorrect. Moreover, do not draw hasty conclusions; ask yourself what you think would make sense to an objective observer. For example, despite his overall good attendance record, Joe arrives late twice in the same week. If Tim bases his perception solely on Joe's behaviors this week, he will say that Joe tends to be tardy and disorganized.

f) Remind yourself that you don't perceive things as they really are (and neither do others). On the contrary, information is selected, organized, and interpreted by your brain to satisfy your needs and confirm your attitudes. The perceived world is not the real world. Give people the benefit of the doubt.

g) Remind yourself that situations are neutral and that it's your interpretation of the situation that creates problems for you. Recognize that errors and distortions arise from the thoughts that you have about a situation and that they do not represent the situation itself. The situation itself is neutral. It becomes positive or negative depending on the label you put on it. So, don't take everything personally, and don't assume that someone intends to attack you or insult you.

h) Try to perceive things accurately. We all have a personal frame of reference that filters all the sensory data that we receive (what we see, hear, feel, smell, and taste). This frame of reference is influenced by several factors such as our needs, our past experiences, our self-esteem, and our personal traits. In judging another person, you might ask, "Is my frame of reference clouding my vision of the 'real' person and how he's behaving right now?" Become aware of what's in your frame and how it's limiting your perspective of the situation. Also, set aside your own frame to grasp the other person's frame.

i) Look at situations from a variety of perspectives. Consider multiple internal and external factors that might influence your successes and failures, and those of others in situations.

j) Stop worrying about what might happen. If you're feeling stressed, your perceptions and thoughts will be especially distorted. Take a break to calm down and breathe if you feel particularly stressed or upset. When you're calm and relaxed, you'll be in a better position to deal with a situation.

k) Identify fair and balanced thoughts. For example, instead of seeing everything in black and white (You're either stupid, or you're amazing), try to be more nuanced (You're very good, but you should work on certain things to get even better). Challenge your errors and distortions and replace them with realistic thoughts.

l) Think about what you could do about the situation. By having a more balanced perspective, the situation may lose importance, and you may decide that you don't need to take special steps to resolve it. Realize that most of the things that people worry about don't happen.

m) Create positive affirmations that you can use to counter errors and distortions in the future. For example, instead of saying "I'm incompetent," say "I'm still learning."

7. **Don't play the blame game.** Ah, the blame game. What fun! Unless we're being blamed for someone else's mistakes, that is! It's important to be aware of how you usually explain what happens to you. If you typically don't recognize your innate responsibility for your own life and what's happening in it, you're likely to develop a feeling of helplessness or even fatalism. And you tend to blame others for anything that goes wrong.

On the other hand, are you the master of your life? Do you take responsibility for what's happening to you, including your successes and failures? These two outlooks on life spell the difference between an external locus of control (thinking that what happens to you doesn't depend on you but, instead, on external factors that are out of your control) and an internal locus of control (attributing the events of your life to personal responsibility). You can determine where you are

on this continuum by paying attention to your self-talk (what you say to yourself). Here are some tips:
a) Notice how often you justify or explain your behavior, a situation, or your success or failure (or that of others) using words such as because, due to, since that's why, the reason being, it was caused by, thanks to, because of, etc.
b) Assume responsibility for yourself, for what happens to you, and for your decisions. Take action to improve your lot in life. Find elements in situations over which you do have control, especially if you tend to blame external factors for what happens to you. At the same time, if you think that you're responsible for EVERYTHING, even stuff that's way beyond your control, stop it! Don't overestimate the scope of your control. Don't take everything on your shoulders.
c) Encourage others to take responsibility by not blaming, rescuing, or placating them. Establish relationships on an equal footing with others, neither above nor below them.
d) Avoid the self-serving bias: a tendency to attribute your successes to internal, personal factors such as ability, intelligence, and hard work, and your failures to unfavorable external factors such as a lack of resources, bad weather, others' incompetence, etc. If what you say is peppered with excuses, look for patterns in the types of excuses you make and find alternatives to them.
e) Avoid committing the fundamental attribution error: a tendency to attribute others' behavior primarily to internal, personal factors and underestimate contextual or situational factors that may be influencing their behavior, for example, attributing someone's lateness to their lack of organizational skills rather than considering the possibility that an accident blocked traffic.

f) Be aware that you have choices. There's always a way for you to regain control by choosing your actions and thoughts. Wellness coach Elizabeth Scott says, "When you realize that you always have the choice to change your situation (even if this change isn't your first choice or is merely a change in how you look at things), it can be liberating and empowering."

g) Brainstorm your options (without stopping to evaluate them) when you feel stuck in a situation. Scott says that this list "can help remind you of your choices and keep you from feeling trapped. It can remind you of what you CAN control, even when many things are set." If helpful, ask a friend to help you brainstorm ideas and select those that are likely to be most effective for you.

8

Relax and Enjoy

Checkmarks! Tim was reviewing his tool sheets and saw lots of checkmarks beside the tips he used. "Cool. I'm finally moving on to Tool 8," Tim said to himself, and he peeked into Roxanne's office.

"Congratulations, Tim. You've worked hard," Roxanne said as Tim showed her his tool sheets, "If you conquered Tool 7, then Tool 8 might be a gentle summer breeze for you."

"Yes, I've been reading the Tool 8 sheets. You know, I'm not really a Zen person; I'm a go-getter. So, all this relaxation stuff might be harder than it looks. I know what you're going to say – do it one step at a time at my own speed."

"Exactly. Have you heard Stephen Covey's story about 'sharpening the saw'? ("Nooo…") To put it briefly, two woodcutters are working hard, but one takes regular breaks. Which one is more productive? ("I would imagine that it's the one who's going at it nonstop.") Nope. It's the one who's taking breaks to refuel himself and sharpen his saw. So, the time that you take to relax and build your energy reserves makes you more effective as a person."

"That makes sense, of course. Unfortunately, I tend to keep on going like an Energizer bunny. Miles to go before I sleep. That sort of thing."

"Hmm…you know how your cell phone indicates how much juice is left in the battery before you have to charge it? Well, our bodies also have an indicator that tells us that it's time to recharge our batteries. And it's important not to ignore those indicators or run our batteries low all the time. We have to pay attention to these signals."

"Oh yes, I read about this in the Tool sheets. My major sign is that I get 'hangry.' My stomach churns, my mood darkens, and I feel drained."

"If you catch the early warning signs and implement your favorite destressing solutions, you'll regain your sense of serenity faster."

"Roxanne, that's common sense and yet not common practice. It's so easy to let stress invade our lives through our habits, our ways of thinking, increasing complexity (our choice), situations where we feel powerless or hopeless, accumulating possessions that become burdens more than blessings, frenziness, you name it. And yet, we (and I mean 'I') wait till it's a good time to relax. 'One day, I'll have the time to take it easy,' I tell myself, and yet that day never comes. The goalposts change: once I achieve a goal (for example, a certain income level), then I aim higher and higher with no end. I never arrive at a point where I can relax."

"As you've probably concluded, Tim, if you wait to have everything sorted and organized and minimalized before you feel free and at peace, you may wait forever."

"Exactly, I need to make relaxation a priority STAT."

Make relaxation a priority STAT!

~ ~ ~

With that, Tim strolled into his office and re-read the Tool 8 sheets. He then rated his overall level of 'relaxation and enjoyment.' He set a goal of achieving a score of at least '7' before moving on to Tool 9. And he followed the same approach that he used with Tool 7: he read the sheets first thing in the morning every day, and, at the end of each day, he placed a checkmark beside the tips he used and an 'x' beside those he botched.

Relaxing didn't come naturally to Tim. It felt so… unproductive. At first, all he could manage were 10-minute chunks of peacefulness. It seems that 'something always happened' that crumbled his sense of calm. However, over time, those chunks grew to 1 hour, then 3 hours, and then, eventually, the entire day – even on a workday! Finally, his sheets were full of checkmarks, and one day, while looking in the bathroom mirror, Tim noticed that he had lost a brick on his back. Whew! A weight has been lifted!

Tool 8 – Relax and Enjoy

"People who always perceived their daily life to be over-the-top stressful were three times more likely to die over the period of study than people who rolled with the punches and didn't find daily life very stressful." – Carolyn Aldwin, director of the Center for Healthy Aging Research

"Every now and then, go away, have a little relaxation, for when you come back to your work, your judgment will be surer. Go some distance away because then the work appears smaller and more of it can be taken in at a glance, and a lack of harmony and proportion is more readily seen." – Leonardo Da Vinci

"Spending more time with friends and family costs nothing. Nor does walking, cooking, meditating, making love, reading, or eating dinner at the table instead of in front of the television. Simply resisting the urge to hurry is freeing." – Carl Honoré

"[I slow down by] taking my dog for a long walk, burying my head in a good book for hours on end, and drinking a cup of coffee while watching the sunrise. I'm learning to look up and not down. I am more intentional with the free time that I have in my day, and I make sure that those moments don't go to waste." –Jennifer Chan

Slow down ~ Let go ~ Sanctuary ~ Rest period ~ Self-care ~ 5Sx2

- ☑ Slow down the speed of your life.
- ☑ Let go and put things in perspective.
- ☑ Create your sanctuary.
- ☑ Take a break and relax.
- ☑ Take care of yourself.
- ☑ Know your 5S x 2: your 5 early warning signs of stress and your 5 best strategies for coping with stress.

Tool 8 –Roxanne's Tips

1. Slow down the speed of your life. Sometimes, we rush through our lives so quickly that we don't experience it. We don't take the time to appreciate the wonderful moments –even the joy of eating a meal without the pressure of deadlines or activities or the all-consuming drone of the television. Think of the many little ways that you tend to rush through your day and find ways to slow the pace.

2. Let go and put things in perspective. Laura Small, an advertising agency VP, says that it's so easy to "catalog countless rejections, real and imagined slights, beefs with co-workers, frustrations, aggravations, and gripes." She suggests that we simply let it go or, if important, go ahead and address it, but "do so calmly, and with a clear understanding of what you want the outcome to be." Some things that seem important right now turn out to be completely unimportant in the long term. Ask yourself, "Will this be important in 10 years?" Moreover, there are things that we can control and act on, and things that we cannot control and should

not act on. As you can see on the following personal power grid developed by burnout researchers Dennis Jaffee and Cynthia Scott, there are two continuums: how much control we have in a situation versus how to respond in the situation.

	Can be Controlled	Risk Zone	Can't be Controlled
Take Action	Situation Mastery		Ceaseless Striving
Don't Act	Giving Up		Letting Go

According to Jaffee and Scott, taking action is appropriate only when you can control a situation. This is an example of situation mastery. You engage in ceaseless striving when you try to take action concerning things that you cannot control. For example, this might occur when you're trying to change someone else's behavior. They must want to change their behavior for change to happen. You're giving up when you don't take action concerning things that you can control. This might happen when you allow others to make decisions for you, when you feel helpless or hopeless in a situation, or when you simply conform to popular opinion rather than take risks.

The flipside of situation mastery is letting go, which is appropriate when you don't have control, and you don't take action. This is a challenging but important skill to learn. As Denis Gaumond, a retired UQAM professor, says: "The more I advance in life, the more I allow myself to simply drop along the path the baggage that no longer belongs to me, that weighs me down and slow down my step, and that prevents me from walking, dancing, singing, and increasing my freedom." You've probably realized that 'situation control' and 'letting go' allow you to make the best use of your time. Choose your battles, and you may win more often!

If you're having trouble letting go, the following rules may be helpful:

- Rule 1: Don't sweat the small stuff: You need to prioritize and identify the things that are worth worrying about and worry about those, but not excessively. Worry doesn't improve situations; constructive problem-solving does! Figure out what's important and remember not to let the small stuff get to you.
- Rule 2: It's all small stuff: Take care of yourself, keep things in perspective, and let go of anxiety. Lots of stuff that we worry about doesn't matter in the long run. If you don't have your health, it doesn't matter how many important things you think you have to do; they won't get accomplished. Nothing is worth compromising your health when it comes right down to it.
- Rule 3: If you can't fight or flee, flow: When it's worth the fight (for example, something that has a huge impact on you or others), you must take some kind of action (not necessarily fighting, though). However, if you cannot fight, flee, or release energy, then let it be and flow. Go with the flow, not against the current.

In any situation, try to find the part over which you have some control, even when you think you have no control. Venture out of any limiting beliefs you have and try new things within your risk zone (where things are only somewhat within your control). Here's an example: while at the airport, Roxanne heard that her flight was delayed by two hours due to weather conditions. How did Roxanne react? She didn't take out her frustration on others. She tried to let go and shift her focus from feeling frustrated to accepting that she can't control the weather, nor can anyone else. She took a few deep breaths, called people awaiting her arrival at her destination, went for a walk, talked with other stranded passengers, and read a new book that she brought along.

With practice, knowing what part of a situation, if any, you can control may become automatic. Here are two principles that can help you stay the course in terms of self-discipline.

a) First, start with the end in mind. This is one of Stephen Covey's seven habits of highly effective people. Before starting a project or your day, you need to have a clear idea of what you want to achieve in the short, medium, and long term. Covey insists that every single choice influences the achievement of our goals. So, when you're tempted to go for another coffee break instead of working, think about how your current actions will influence your future. Having a clear idea of what you want also allows you to make more thoughtful choices that match your priorities and show respect for yourself. Thinking about what accomplishing your goal will represent will help you be more motivated to move in that direction without getting distracted. The question to ask yourself is, "Did my choices today move me toward attaining my goals?"

b) The second principle is to surround yourself with the right people who will help you stay the course. If you want to achieve a specific goal or live the life you want, ensure that you have people around you who will support and challenge you to reach your goal. These people make up your 'team' in life, so choose them carefully. Moreover, if you make people aware of your goals (in other words, publicly commit to your goals), giving up on them will become harder (and possibly embarrassing). For example, telling your coworkers that, from now on, you will stop checking your cell phone every few minutes during a meeting may help you feel more accountable for following through on your promise. Unfortunately, we are more likely to keep promises that we make to others than to ourselves. Is this true for you?

3. Create your personal relaxation sanctuary. Your sanctuary is a place that you can go to – either physically or mentally – where you let your guard down, relax, and be quiet without interruptions or noise from the outside world. For example, a garden, a particular room in your home, or a park. Belinda Crestani, a lifestyle and wellness writer, suggests that you "go there as needed to collect your thoughts, decompress and practice that deep breathing and positive self-talk."

4. Take a break and relax. However tempting it may be to simply skip breaks and keep on working, you're better off taking one. Rather than taking time away from work, relaxing breaks actually reduce mental fatigue and increase brain functioning

and productivity, according to research by neuroscientist Adam Gazzaley and psychologist Larry Rosen. But the break should be restorative, such as a 10-minute walk, talk (not about work), or meditation. Here are some possibilities:

a) Disconnect. According to psychologist Larry Rosen, accessing your cell phone does NOT constitute a *genuine* break. Nor do watching TV or YouTube, accessing social media, or searching the Internet, for that matter. Also, to encourage conversation, agree with others to create an area where cell phones are not allowed, such as the dinner table or the meeting room. Consider applying a penalty for each time a cell phone is accessed during dinner (for example, paying for everyone's meal if at a restaurant).

b) Walk. Walking is a simple, easy, zero-cost activity that can help you recharge your batteries. In their research, Stanford researchers Marily Oppezzo and Daniel Schwartz found that walking outdoors significantly increased participants' creativity. Challenge yourself to walk a certain number of steps (for example, 10,000 steps) every day. Use the pedometer on your cell phone to track your results.

c) Power nap. Figure out what length of nap helps you feel refreshed and not groggy. You can experiment with a power nap (10 to 20 minutes) or a nano-nap (2 to 5 minutes). Sleep researchers Rajiv Dhand, Olaf Lahl, and others at the National Institute of Mental Health have established the benefits of naps, including increased alertness, better performance, improved memory, and reduced information overload. There are even apps available to help you nap. Find a dark, quiet place where you're unlikely to be interrupted and, perhaps, place a 'Do not disturb' sign on your office door. Remember to mute your cell phone and set an alarm so that you don't oversleep. If you're having trouble falling asleep, you can try Dr. Weil's 4-7-8 breathing exercise in which you:  (a) exhale through your mouth, then (b) inhale through your nose for a count of 4, then (c) hold your breath for a count of 7, and then (d) exhale through your mouth for a count of 8 (while making a whooshing sound). Repeat three more times. Another option is to count backward from 100, starting back at 100 if you forget where you are. According to hypnotherapist Phillip Mandel, visualizing the numbers makes this sleep-inducer even more effective.

d) Meditate. There are many forms of meditation (contemplative prayer, mindfulness meditation, Christian meditation, silent prayer, etc.). It's a matter of finding one that works for you and sticking with it since the benefit s may not be immediately noticeable. And sometimes the benefits are more noticeable to others than to you. An option is to do a walking meditation, which is a long, quiet walk, preferably in a natural setting. Lots of websites and smartphone apps are available to help you meditate at home or anywhere you go.

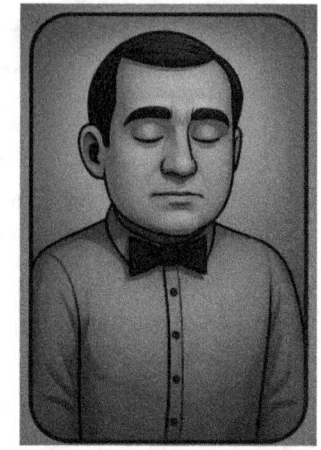

5. Take care of yourself. You can become more resilient in the face of stress by adopting a healthy lifestyle. As lifestyle advocate D. Poupard suggests, this involves eating well (including breakfast and unprocessed foods), sleeping well (at least seven to eight hours each night), drinking plenty of water, maintaining healthy and fulfilling relationships, exercising (180 minutes of cardiovascular and strength training per week), relaxing, completing unfinished projects, being organized, and rewarding yourself with small rewards every day. That sounds like a lot, but it's doable – one choice at a time.

6. Know your 5S x 2: your 5 early warning signs of stress and your 5 strategies for coping with stress.
    a) Figure out your 5 early warning signs. Understanding what stress means to you personally allows you to quickly recognize its presence, identify the most effective ways to cope with it, and become aware of the factors that lead to its occurrence. According to the Center for Studies on Human Stress, NUTS is the universal recipe for stress: the situation is New to you, it's Unpredictable, it Threatens your ego, and you don't feel a Sense of control.

Do you recognize stress when it knocks on your door? What are *your* five biggest early signs of stress? How do you feel (anxious, irritable, impatient, sad, etc.)? What are your thoughts (negative attitudes, lack of concentration)? How do you feel stress in your body (insomnia, decreased energy, headaches)? What do you tend to do when you're stressed (isolating, decreasing productivity, eating, being critical or unappreciative)? When we experience high levels of stress, it can be hard to have the presence of mind to recognize that we are indeed experiencing stress and to adopt measures to decrease our stress. So recognizing it is vital.

b) The next step is identifying your 5 favorite ways of reducing your stress level. These actions help you recharge your batteries and calm you down. Even small things can make a difference in how you feel. Here are some examples:
- → going for a long walk
- → chatting with a friend
- → cooking your favorite meal
- → sitting on a bench and observing your surroundings
- → taking a nap
- → reading a good book
- → playing with your pet
- → doing a hobby such as gardening or woodworking
- → meditating

Experiment and figure out which combinations of actions are most effective in reducing your stress. If you have a list of solutions for overcoming stress at hand, you will be able to de-stress more quickly.

9

Eliminate People Clutter

"Roxanne!" Tim called out as he read the heading of the Tool 9 sheet and stepped into Roxanne's office. "Woohoo! Now I get to get rid of people who clutter up my life. This reminds me of the movie *Up in the Air*. Remember it? ("Yes…") Well, the character played by George Clooney, a guy who specializes in firing people, gives motivational speeches on what people carry in their metaphorical backpacks. He invites people to fill their backpacks with acquaintances, family, friends, coworkers, and whoever else is in their lives, and then feel how heavy it is ('how the straps cut into your shoulders'). He says, 'All those negotiations and arguments, and secrets and compromises: you don't need to carry all that weight. Why don't you set that bag down?' He argues that relationships are a burden; that they limit a person's freedom. And the best scenario is to maximize one's independence by avoiding them. Indeed, he says that he doesn't do 'ships – relation-ships!'"

"Tim, that may be what he says, but at the end of the movie, we discover that he lives a lonely life with few attachments and little meaning."

"Ah...okay, that's sad. I only want to get rid of the people who aren't useful to me. You know, those who are a drag to be around, those who don't contribute to my personal growth, happiness, and –"

"Hmm...I think that we shouldn't simply maintain relationships with people based on how they may be of use to us and then 'throw them away' once we're done with them. 'Love people, use things' suggest the minimalists, Joshua and Ryan. Carol McCloud makes this point nicely in her children's book *Have You Filled a Bucket Today?* 'We all carry an invisible bucket in which we keep our good thoughts and feelings. When our buckets are full, we are happy; when they are empty, we are sad. We can fill our own bucket, and so can others. We can also dip into it. Bucket fillers are those who help without being asked, give hugs and compliments, and generally spread their love and good feelings to others. People who dip into our bucket often rob us of happy feelings by refusing to help with a task or by saying or doing cruel things.' What about you, are you a bucket filler or a dipper?"

Have you filled a bucket today?

"Oh, now that you put it this way, I guess I've been doing a bit of dipping. Well, what does people clutter mean anyway? I have to say that I'm exhausted from the politics and conflict and general conniving around here."

"Tim, people clutter is the interpersonal stuff that gets in the way of...everything. For example, personal battles, the stings from being excluded, the slings and arrows of rivalries, cliques, and struggles to get to the top of the hill, trying to please everyone, backstabbing, gossip, politics, etc. There's no way to eliminate them, but you can set some boundaries around you that protect you from this morass of slithering snakes and broken ladders...so to speak."

"Sounds good. So, if I understand correctly, eliminating people clutter means creating peaceful and mutually respectful relationships with others. Where do I start?"

"First, realize that everything you've done so far to adopt minimalism at work will help you stay grounded and less frazzled by interpersonal issues. You need to keep using those tools and adapting them as needed. Second, be conscientious about your performance levels: be organized, self-disciplined, and perform at a high level. Follow through on your commitments, and –"

"Oh, so if I deal with non-people issues well, then my work – and I – won't be a target or lightning rod for others. This sets the stage for dealing with people clutter. Hmmm, but what about politics? If I refuse to play the game, won't I be played by the game? Quite frankly, one of my problems has been that I don't know the rules of the game. They're unwritten and in the hands of the chosen few, so it's been hard for me to know how to play the game, not to mention play it well."

"Being a game player requires that you invest lots of time, focus, and energy in reading situations and developing alliances with 'the right people.' And yes, there are definite risks to not playing the game at all. If you opt out, you don't get easy access to privileges that those in the inner circle have. And you'll feel a tinge of disillusionment (or more) when you see someone less competent than you receive special advantages. Frankly, Tim, this happens more often than I can shake a stick at. But, make no mistake, there are costs associated with being a game player. These folks have a habit of leaving a trail of damaged relationships and I.O.U.s behind them and becoming easy targets. They tend to rise to their point of incompetence ("Oh, I think that's the Peter principle."), and they spend their time dealing with politics, manipulating, and back-scratching, all the while compromising their values. They may seem to have it all handed to them on a silver platter, but with everything they have received, there are expectations that they will return the favor. Eventually, I think it all catches up to them in one way or another…"

"So, playing the game is profitable but also costly. I can't imagine how I can be calm while creating alliances and double-crossing people when it's advantageous to me. I've watched Survivor, and I've seen the trail of destruction that this leaves. Besides, it would take lots of energy and would be stressful. So, I'd like to stay in the game but play it by my own rules. So, what do I do instead?"

"Being agreeable and adaptable (being flexible rather than rigid) with well-defined limits is what I suggest. Be someone who stays above the fray and doesn't attract negative attention. Know when to say 'yes' and know when to say 'no,' but, especially, know when to say nothing. Don't get involved in others' squabbles. ("Should I be neutral like Switzerland?") People will try to draw you into their tiffs and causes, but the minute that you support some people, you position yourself in opposition to others – in the parlance of office politics."

"Oh, maybe I should avoid people altogether. You know, just be distant and reserved. Right now, unfortunately, I'm really in the middle of it all: I know everyone's business, and they know mine. Want to hear some juicy tidbits about Joe?"

"No thanks, Tim. Going from one extreme to another, like a slingshot, rarely works. The central theme of Tool 9 is placing a solid but flexible boundary around you."

"Oh, like Les Nessman on the show *WKRP in Cincinnati*, who put masking tape on the floor around him…but figuratively?"

"Ah, not quite. The best way to picture this is a type of continuum."

And with this, Roxanne took out a sheet of paper and drew the following table as she explained its elements.

"According to psychotherapist Charles Whitfield, you can be too independent AND dependent. There are extremely independent folks who have a wall around them. Their boundary is rigid and impermeable. They don't let people in and are detached and distant from others."

"That doesn't sound like much fun. It would be solitary and kind of lonely."

"Then, jumping past The Zone, there are folks who are overly dependent on others and who tend to have a blurred or weak boundary between themselves and others. They soak up others' opinions and issues. They are too involved in others' lives, just as others are overly drawn into their lives."

"That sounds familiar. I'm a people pleaser at heart. I don't want to disappoint other people, so I have trouble saying 'no.' Because of this, I'm overloaded with work, and other people's problems and expectations are swimming laps around my mind. I drop what I'm doing to help others. And they know this and take advantage of it."

"That sounds uncomfortable, Tim. You may want to pull the plug and drain the stuff."

"So, what do we do about people who are constantly invading our boundaries, you know, the complainers, the victims who refuse to do anything about their situations, the naggers, the people who take advantage of us, the people who drain our energy, the domineering jerks, the bullies? At what point should we decide that a relationship isn't working, and limit or stop being in contact with those people?"

"Tim, once you begin managing your boundaries, you'll find that some people will start interacting with you in a reasonable manner and others will stop interacting with you altogether because you're no longer playing their game. But that's not always the case for everyone: some people will keep pushing and pushing till they get what they want. Their patterns of behavior are ingrained and seem to work with others. And, yes, you may need to reduce the amount of contact that you have with certain people by keeping your interactions brief or less frequent. Stephanie Culp calls this 'people purging' and she goes even

WAY TOO MUCH INDEPENDENCE!	The Zone Just the right amount of independence + dependence	WAY TOO MUCH DEPENDENCE!
Rigid boundary Walled' in Disconnected Alienated Avoidant Distancing Closed Mistrusting Counter-dependence	**HEALTHY BOUNDARY** Flexible & Firm as desired Distance | Involvement Privacy —⋀— Sharing (Balanced) Autonomous but connected Respectful (non-invasive) Responsible for self Calm Meets own needs Self-set & managed Open to others + their opinions, but makes their own (reasoned) choices Clear boundary (to self + others)	Blurred boundary Neglects own needs Clinging Overinvolved Attached at the hip People-pleasing Individuality Caught up in others' issues Fusion Dependent on others' acceptance & approval

further and suggests that you completely eliminate interactions with some people. I have reduced to almost zero the number of interactions that I have with toxic people."

"Cool. So, what's The Zone about?"

"As you can see, neither of the extremes works. The best boundary, The Zone, is set by yourself and is flexible or firm, depending on what works for you in a given situation. So you're both independent and dependent, but the dosage is just right for you. When you're in The Zone, you're taking care of your needs, but you're also involved and engaged with others without being dependent on them. When people are trying to become less dependent, they often 'slingshot' to extreme independence – and vice versa."

"That sounds like a delicate balance. How do I make the journey from Blurred Boundaries to The Zone? And will people be mad at me?"

"Yes, there will be ~~some~~ lots of push-back from people who are used to experiencing you as an ultra-compliant person – initially. Some people may be downright angry about your 'sudden stubbornness' ("What's gotten into you?" they'll ask.) and try to convince you of the error of your ways. You're changing the 'terms of your relationship' after all. But eventually, they'll accept your new boundaries. The first step is finding yourself on the continuum, which I think you've already done. Next, I think that Tool 9 will help you make the leap to The Zone. These tips worked for me, and you might find them useful. Let's look at them together."

~ ~ ~

And with that, Tim and Roxanne reviewed the Tool sheets and discussed his options. Of all the tools in the toolbox, this one posed the greatest challenge for Tim. A natural people pleaser with outstretched arms to everyone around him, Tim often found himself in the middle of others' interpersonal drama, listening to complaints, sharing confidences, forming alliances, and, sadly, being played even by those he trusted the most when it was opportune for them to do so. All of this stress took its toll on Tim: he had trouble sleeping and his thoughts were consumed by interpersonal issues and slights. He felt hurt, confused, and used.

With Roxanne's help, Tim decided to analyze his work relationships. He made a list of the names of people that he interacted with regularly, starting with the most important relationships. Then, he rated the quality of his interactions with them from 1 (poor, strained, negative) to 10 (supportive, positive, respectful). After analyzing the results, he considered how to invest more in important relationships and troubleshoot any problematic relationships that make his work life difficult. With some super-toxic colleagues, just like Roxanne, he decided to maintain professional but distant relationships.

Over time, Tim drew a (figurative) boundary around himself, put some distance between himself and the game, built close but not enmeshed relationships with his key contacts (people with whom he wanted to build stronger relationships), and adopted a pleasant but 'above the fray' demeanor at work (being kind to everyone but with limits that he chose for himself). At times, he felt like he was a red-hot coal that was losing its access to oxygen (drama). Instead of fueling it, he was gradually sliding a cover over it, removing its oxygen. It was painful, but his leap out of the fire allowed him to breathe easier. He began to feel less stressed, and, eventually, a brick slid off his back. He was almost free of his load of bricks. Only a few bricks remained!

Tool 9 – Eliminate People Clutter

"Do all the good you can, by all the means you can, in all the ways you can, in all the places you can, at all the times you can, to all the people you can, as long as ever you can." – John Wesley

"Relax. Be present. Listen deeply. Be positive. Speak warmly. Slowly. Briefly." – Andrew Newberg & Mark Waldman

"Encouragement to others is something everyone can give. Somebody needs what you have to give. It may not be your money; it may be your time. It may be your listening ear. It may be your arms to encourage. It may be your smile to uplift. Who knows?" – Joel Osteen

"Sorting out and letting go of what is not ours is often easier than sorting and owning what is actually ours...What helps me differentiate these two –my stuff and your stuff –are healthy boundaries...When I truly let go of something that is toxic or not mine anyway, I no longer beat myself up about it, thus freeing me to experience a more successful and enjoyable life." – Charles Whitfield

"People have an emotional bank account for each relationship; we make deposits when we are trusting, empathetic, and dependable. We make withdrawals when we are inconsiderate, dishonest, and arbitrary. When our accounts become overdrawn, we have to be especially careful about everything we say in case it is misinterpreted. It leads to defensiveness in which people are most concerned about defending themselves." - Stephen Covey

"Seeking to please is a perilous trap." –Epictetus

"To make life more bearable and pleasant for everybody, choose the issues that are significant enough to fight over, and ignore or use distraction for those you can let slide that day. Picking your battles will eliminate a number of conflicts and yet will still leave you feeling in control." –Lawrence Balter

"You are – in some or many ways – just like the people you spend the most time with…Who you share your world with is up to you. Hang around positive people who look for the good and you can't help but do the same because you do become who your friends are… If you consistently come away feeling bad after talking or being with a particular person, you've somehow fallen into a negative trap and the only way out is to stop talking for a while…Just stop until you can get yourself in a better place and learn some techniques to keep you from diving back into the mud pits." – Paula Renaye

"Don't hang around people who are consistently engaging in conflict … People who regularly fight with others will eventually fight with you." – Naval Ravikant

"There are some people who always seem angry and continuously look for conflict. Walk away from these people. The battle they're are fighting isn't with you, it's with themselves." –Rashida Rowe

"Remember: You will never earn the same rewards as others without employing the same methods and investment of time as they do. It is unreasonable to think we can earn rewards without being willing to pay their true price." –Epictetus

"Never depend on the admiration of others. There is no strength in it. Personal merit cannot be derived from an external source." –Epictetus

"Just because someone throws you a ball doesn't mean you have to catch it. ....If your focus is on being the best you and doing your very best in every situation, everything else will fall into place – even if the ball-throwers find someone else to play catch with." – Paula Renaye

Perform ~ Respect ~ Professional ~ Positive ~ Appreciate ~ Give ~ Include ~ Boundaries ~ Stay Above the Fray ~ Understand ~ Admit Mistakes ~ Don't Generate Conflict ~ Dodge the Horsemen

- ☑ Perform and help others succeed.
- ☑ Maintain appropriate boundaries.
- ☑ Demonstrate respect for others.
- ☑ Maintain pleasant and professional relationships.
- ☑ Compliment others.
- ☑ Be a giver, not a taker.
- ☑ Include everyone in your in-group.
- ☑ Stay above the fray.
- ☑ Seek to understand others first.
- ☑ Admit your mistakes and be calm when dealing with others' foibles.
- ☑ Don't generate conflict.
- ☑ Keep the four horsemen out of your interactions.

Tool 9 – Roxanne's Tips

In his article, *Vice and Virtue in Everyday Life*, ethics professor Douglas Chismar proposes that our day-to-day civilities are a broader reflection of the quality of our character. Some of the tips below include his rules of social etiquette and ideas from Stephen Covey's book *Principle-Centered Leadership*.

1. Perform and help others succeed. Be a solid contributor who has good relationships with everyone. Deliver what you promise on time and without hassles. Maintain a solid reputation. This will prevent you from attracting negative attention.

2. Maintain appropriate boundaries:
   a) Find out where The Zone is for you. Check out the diagram on page 92, figure out where you are, where you want to be, and how to bridge the gap. The tips in this section will help you bridge the gap.
   b) Don't be a people pleaser: learn to say no politely and firmly. You simply cannot please everyone. Don't make others responsible for your own feelings ("You make me feel …"). Attempts to make you feel guilty or inadequate will not work without your cooperation. Don't shield people from their bad behavior. Don't agree to cover up inappropriate behaviors or help people hide their errors and omissions.
   c) Be assertive using the three Fs: state the Facts of what happened, describe your Feelings (the impact of what happened on you), and then explain what you want and need in the Future in a non-threatening way.
   d) Follow Paula Renaye's advice: "Take the 'kick me' sign off your back. If you feel like people take advantage of you all the time, you are not a victim, you are a volunteer... Putting up

with unacceptable behavior doesn't make you 'good,' it makes you a doormat. When you respect yourself, others will too. If you want different outcomes, make different choices." In managing your boundaries, Paula Renaye suggests that you ask yourself a few questions: "Would a person with high self-esteem and self-respect do what I'm doing? Consider what I'm considering? Think what I'm thinking? Tolerate what I'm tolerating?"

3. Demonstrate respect for others. Keep appointments and be punctual. Don't make others wait for you to show up or be ready. Reliability is a sign of respect. Read your emails and return calls promptly (usually within 24 hours). Return what you borrow (pens, files, catalogs). Refill the coffee pot, the copy machine, and the gas tank of the company car. Clean up after yourself. No one should ever have the impression that you're so self-centered that you're leaving a mess for them.

4. Maintain pleasant and professional relationships with all:
   a) Be reserved, instead of entangled: don't get overly involved in other people's *stuff*, whether it's personal or professional.
   b) Build relationships one pleasant interaction at a time. Simply being nice to others goes a long way to preventing conflict. Don't leave a trail of broken relationships behind you (and don't try to cover your tracks). Instead, take ownership of your part in a misunderstanding and reach out to others.
   c) Support your boss. Figure out your boss's key interests and work towards them. Don't make your boss look like an idiot in front of others or badmouth your boss when their back is turned. Payback is certain.
   d) Be cooperative. Instead of insisting that you get your way, agree with others as much as possible (unless what they are proposing is unethical, immoral, or illegal).

e) In a misunderstanding, focus on the problem, not the person, or your dislike or disrespect for them. Obtain specific information – who, what, when, where, and how – and examples of specific behaviors and consequences. Try to understand the interests that are beneath the other person's position. Consider multiple alternatives for resolving issues and look for a win-win solution.

5. Be positive and upbeat. Have a sense of humor. Don't dwell on or talk about negative things. Stay cool as a cucumber. It's better to smile and stay quiet than to scowl and mouth off (and live to regret it). People prefer to be around positive people who don't drag them down into the dumpster with their miserable attitudes. There is often a bright side to most issues. If you can't find a constructive angle to a contentious issue, it is often best to stay quiet.

6. Compliment others and celebrate their successes! Find a way to express your appreciation, congratulate, or compliment others. Even a brief email will do! As Leo Buscaglia says, "Too often we underestimate the power of a touch, a smile, a kind word, a listening ear, an honest compliment, or the smallest act of caring, all of which have the potential to turn a life around." Put others in the spotlight rather than yourself. Give credit where it's due: don't use others' ideas without giving credit.

7. Be a giver, not a taker. In his book, *Give and Take*, psychologist Adam Grant talks about three kinds of people:
    a. Takers are strategic in their relationships with others. These self-focused people would rather receive than give. In fact, for them, relationships are win/lose in a dog-eat-dog world. They are only willing to help others when it clearly benefits them and requires minimal time.

b. Givers are other-focused, generous, and win-win-oriented. They help others without expecting anything in return. Givers may be perceived as doormats, but they do reap the benefits eventually (not to mention the personal peace that comes with giving).
c. Matchers prefer the give-and-take of relationships. They give to others but expect to receive something in return. So, they're calculative and exchange oriented.

According to research, the best approach over the long term is being a giver because it has a ripple effect on others and helps to build solid relationships. However, because some people will take advantage of your generosity, it may be worthwhile to establish limits (boundaries!) with those individuals. In sum, where possible, give others the support and resources they need to do their work well. This will nurture your relationships with them and may motivate them to support you and others in the future.

8. Include everyone in your in-group. Don't ostracize or exclude folks. Never hurt, demean, or be punitive toward people. Show patience and politeness toward others who may not express themselves the same way that you do. Hurting people doesn't teach them a better way; it damages their self-confidence and causes them to see themselves as failures.  Organizational change specialist Marvin Weisbord says that everyone asks themselves, consciously or otherwise, whether

they are more 'in or out.' "The more 'in' we feel, the better we cooperate. The more 'out' we feel, the more we withdraw, work alone, daydream, and defeat ourselves and other people." According to psychologists Roy Baumeister and Mark Leary, the need to belong is fundamental to human existence. So, when you exclude people, you're denying them what is essential to life.

9. Stay above the fray. Avoid political maneuvering, manipulation, rumor-mongering, and game-playing. And avoid getting involved in other people's drama. Instead, be polite, reasonable, and helpful to others. Don't feel that you have to react to everything that doesn't fit with your preferences or to someone pushing your red buttons. Exercise self-control and restraint, especially when you or others are tired or your emotions are frayed. As Paula Renaye says in her book *Living the Life You Love*, "As long as you have buttons, somebody somewhere is going to push them. As long as you automatically respond to particular things in particular ways, you will keep getting those particular experiences." So, have a filter: what's on the tip of your tongue isn't always appropriate to share with others. When you (or others) are hungry, cold, stressed, or tired, you're likely to be reactive and have a short fuse.

10. Seek to understand others first. Try to understand what others are telling you before attempting to be understood. Don't automatically assume that someone has bad intentions. Sometimes, people do things without thinking. Clarify your expectations and understandings, as well as those of others. Ask for clarification: "Did I understand correctly? Did you say...?" Allow others to influence you. If you're closed to others' opinions, you'll come across as having an "I'm right, and you're wrong attitude."

11. Admit your mistakes and be calm and patient when dealing with others' foibles, issues, and bad days. We all make mistakes. We're all in the process of learning.
    a) Don't hide your mistakes or shift the blame or demonize others, but at the same time, don't beat yourself up about them. Instead, take responsibility and admit your errors or your contribution to a misunderstanding when appropriate. More importantly, find solutions for recovering from your errors.
    b) Assume the best of others: give people the benefit of the doubt. You would want them to do this for you, wouldn't you? Be patient with others, especially when you or others are stressed. Don't use threats, pressure, and coercion to get the job done. You might get it done in the short term, but your strong-arming will come back to haunt you.

12. Don't generate conflict. Conflict, competition, and relationship chaos can quickly eat up your time, energy, and spirit.
    a) Don't create drama, complain, or be over-the-top competitive or negative. Don't be drawn into petty accusations or bitter acrimony.
    b) Don't find entertainment in or get involved in others' conflicts. You may soon become the target. In the words of Charles Whitfield, try to "sort out just what is mine and what is not mine, and not get involved in or take on their conflicts."
    c) Encourage people who have complaints about someone else to talk to that person directly. People who speak to you about others are usually quite willing to talk to others about you.
    d) Take the high road. Be constructive. Be proactive instead of reactive; make conscious choices regarding how to act in a situation, rather than simply doing whatever the urge strikes you to do. Deal with issues as they arise; small irritants become big issues if not dealt with promptly. Consider the

following advice from Mary Ann Pietzker: "Before sharing your opinion about something, you should ask yourself four questions: 'Is what I'm about to say kind? Is it true? Is it necessary? Does it improve upon the silence?'" If your answer to these questions is yes, then go ahead and share your opinion.

13. Keep the horsemen out of your interactions. In their research, psychologist John Gottman and his team found that, after observing couples interact with each other for only a matter of seconds, they could predict with 93% accuracy whether the couples were headed for divorce. In particular, they found that contempt, criticism, stonewalling, and defensiveness (the four horsemen) predicted divorce.
    a) When people express contempt, the most serious of the horsemen, they consider themselves better than others. They display disrespect and condescension toward the other person. They may roll their eyes, sneer, mock, or put others down to make them feel small (for example, "You look like hell!").
    b) Criticism consists of excessive, non-constructive negative judgments that are experienced as an attack (for example, "You're so lazy!"). Comments are especially critical when absolute terms such as "You always ..." or "You never ..." are used. Paula Renaye suggests that "The only reason any criticism from any source hurts is because there is a part of you that believes it's true. ...If I say you have green hair, it won't bother you because you know you don't have green hair."
    c) Stonewalling involves giving others the silent treatment, changing the subject, or even withdrawing from the conversation, perhaps by leaving the room. It happens when

a person is overwhelmed with the conversation and needs to distance themselves.

d) Finally, when people are defensive, they place themselves in the role of victim and make excuses or blame the other person for the situation. They don't see how they share responsibility for a problem or situation.

10

Put Work in Perspective

"I thought that the last few tools were challenging, but this one is especially…intense," Tim said to Roxanne as he sank into her visitors' chair. "We've covered lots of ground so far. I've removed clutter from my office, my wardrobe, my commuting, my electronic habits, my time use, my ways of thinking and being, and my relationships. That's a lot."

"Yes, you've done some solid work, and you need to keep at it; decluttering is an ongoing process. Not only is what you've done important in its own right, but it also lays the groundwork for Tool 10."

"Oh, I see. So, the process began with baby steps, so to speak. Had we started with Tool 10, I might have been overwhelmed. Anyhow, I've been reading your Tool 10 sheets. Can you remind me how putting work in perspective relates to minimalism? It seems to me that, if I were a pure minimalist, I might simply drop out of my corporate job, just like minimalists Joshua and Ryan did."

"For some people, that might be the solution to the problem of work taking over every minute of their existence. They might feel numb or lost at work and seek significance elsewhere in their lives. But that's not the case for everyone. Some of us get a lot of meaning from our work, and ~~some~~ most of us need to work to pay the bills. At the same time, we need to rethink our emotional, energy, and time investments in our jobs."

"Oh! Does that mean minimizing our engagement and commitment to our work? You know, doing the minimum needed just to get by?"

"Uh…not quite. Remember, for Joshua and Ryan, 'Minimalism is a tool to rid yourself of life's excess in favor of focusing on what's important—so you can find happiness, fulfillment, and freedom.' So, in terms of our work life, it means asking ourselves some difficult questions, such as the following:

- Why are we working: do we work to live, or do we live to work?
- Are we tethered to our work? For example, are we constantly connected to work voluntarily or involuntarily via cell phones, GPS tracking, or other technology?
- How much of our work seeps into our leisure and family (think not only about time but also energy and emotional reserves)? Do we bring work to dinner with us? Bed?

("Yes...") Leisure time with family?
- Does work or thinking about work dominate our lives? Does it dominate our sense of self and self-worth? Would we feel lost and useless if we didn't have a job?
- How much meaning do we derive from our work? Do we feel like we're making a difference in the lives of others?
- Are we working our job, or is our job working us over?

Our answers to these questions can help us put work in perspective."

"Oh! I'm guilty on all charges! Is that so bad?"

"Tim, only you can answer that question for yourself. Tool 10 offers you a 5-step process for putting your work in perspective, in other words, making work 'work' for you. The process involves lots of thinking and analysis, and you have to be brutally honest with yourself. But by the end of it, you'll be clearer about how to gain a sense of meaning, joy, peace, and freedom at work. As Paula Renaye says, 'When you're actively in charge of your life, you aren't just drifting along, letting things happen, reacting and fighting fires as they come up – what you do has a purpose. When you have a clear goal, you know what will get you closer to it and what won't, and you don't get caught up in distracting dramas or other nonsense. And if you do get triggered, you immediately look for the why and deal with it.'"

"Wow, that's a tall order! But that's what I want ultimately. What if I don't like what I find?"

"Then, you'll have some choices to make. And you'll be better equipped to make those choices."

"Hmm...can't I just let life take me where it wants me to go?"

"Of course, if that's what you really want. This reminds me of what Carol Adrienne wrote in her book, *The Purpose of Your Life*. She said, 'We cannot drift aimlessly – hoping to keep every option open – because we will wind up doing nothing in the name of "being open." It will be necessary to take an initial stand or to choose a focus, and then follow the feedback that comes from doing that. Without some kind of focus, you will not be able to engage your life deeply enough to let the synchronicities take you where you need to go.'"

"True enough. Hmm...I was looking at the Sweet Spot diagram (on page 113), and I must say that the Quadrant 1 folks have it made. I mean, why commit to a company that doesn't commit to you?"

"I understand that point of view. But we spend soooo much of our lives working that I think we should try to find meaning in it. Al Gini, who wrote this amazing book called *My Job, My Self*, says, 'If we are not satisfied with our work…even if this discontent doesn't spill over into our social and family lives – we are, at the very least, unhappy in well over half of our daily existence. …Only if we're lucky will it be pleasant, pay well, and make us happy. The degree to which we can find this combination is the degree to which work, any work, is satisfying.'"

"Ah, good point. Hmm…I'm afraid that I'm mainly in Quadrant 2. Climbing that corporate ladder has its drawbacks. I hope that our boss will appreciate my commitment and give me a raise or a promotion or, ideally, both!"

"So, for you, success means getting promotions?"

"Of course, that's natural, isn't it?"

"That is the traditional perspective of career success, but, according to Mike Driver, a career management specialist, there are multiple career paths, all of which are equally valuable:

- **Linears**, who, like you, equate career success with gaining power and status and rising through the ranks.
- **Steady-state experts** (professionals and trades) who take lots of pride in their skills and are perfectly happy doing the same things continually, as long as they're doing a good job. Promoting them to a managerial job takes them away from their core competence.
- **Spirals** who adore creativity and new ideas, new experiences, and learning. They will trade power for the opportunity to do something new and interesting.
- **Transitories** who see work as a means to an end – gaining enough money to do the things they really want to do."

"Ah, transitories are probably in Quadrant 1, right?"

"You got it. The problem arises when linears think that everyone should see career progress in the same way that they see it. And they make non-linears feel bad for their choices."

"And linears might be in Quadrant 2 or 3?"

"Possibly. For me, it's important that I enjoy my career, not 'survive' it, which is what I think lots of folks are doing ("Ah, playing Survivor at work!"). For everything I do, I ask how it increases my sense of meaning and contribution. I try to find meaning, joy, peace, and freedom NOW, not in some distant future."

"It's hard not to sacrifice the present for the future. I see that your sweet spot is not in Quadrant 3, which I thought was the 'ideal' quadrant."

"Yes, that's what we often hear: organizations want employees who are 100% engaged and committed to them. But I feel that I can still be engaged and committed on my own terms. I agree with Al Gini, who suggests that we should be loyal and committed to ourselves first. I don't put all my eggs in one basket: I feel I work best when I balance my contribution to my job with my contribution to my overall life. What's important to me is keeping my life simple and making a difference for others."

"But, don't you want to be promoted?"

"No, I'm a spiral who loves being creative and having lots of freedom on the job. There's a tradeoff between power and freedom: the higher up you go in an organization, the less freedom and autonomy you have. Just ask yourself, 'Is it worth it to me?' And, as you move up the hierarchy and gain more power, you'll experience more politics and conflict than ever before. You'll be a lightning rod for others' discontent. It comes with the job. And more power and visibility come with higher stress."

"You may have a point. I see how our boss is well paid, but definitely not well enough to justify the added stress and all the hoops he has to jump through to defend our work unit in the organization. Besides, he once told me that he feels like he's a daycare manager because of all the employees coming to him with issues. I've always thought that you had your ducks in a row. But are you like a duck?

You know, 'Above the surface, look composed and unruffled. Below the surface, paddle like hell!'"

"I used to be, but now I'm like a duck in calm waters. And as Adam Johnson wrote in *The Stanford Daily*, ducks seek out calm waters and don't need to paddle relentlessly. I've made the conscious choice to be a high-performing 'backbencher.' I'm not a mover and a shaker, but I'm respected. I don't need status symbols, I don't care about appearances, and I try to be authentic. Of course, the downside is that I ~~may be~~ am left out of important decisions and not given the recognition and opportunities that others receive. But the benefits outweigh the costs for me. You have to decide what works for you. Do you absolutely need a higher salary, increased power, increased work, increased responsibilities, and increased complexities?"

"Hmm…not really. Can we review what I did in the Tool 10 exercises to make sure that I'm on the right track?"

"Sure, let's work through Tool 10 together. As an aside, I hope you found the job crafting exercise to be thought-provoking. I modeled it very loosely after an exercise that Justin Berg, Jane Dutton, and Amy Wrzesniewski created. They consider job crafting to be an opportunity for employees to redefine and reimagine their jobs so that they're more fulfilling and meaningful. In their research, they found that job crafting made a big difference in levels of satisfaction and meaning at work."

~ ~ ~

And then, Tim and Roxanne turned their attention to his completed Tool 10 sheets. After discussing all the worksheets and highlighted pages of notes, some patterns revealed themselves.

Although Tim's current job wasn't an ideal match to his Wish List, he found ways to make his work more meaningful and less taxing. He pushed away the less important and less fulfilling tasks, redefined important but less interesting tasks, and created meaningful tasks that jived with his Wish List.

The process wasn't easy, but at the same time, it wasn't as hard as he thought it would be. He only wished that he had done it sooner. He didn't realize how freeing it would feel to have absolutely no bricks on his back.

Tool 10 – Put Work in Perspective

"Most people do not accumulate a body of experience. Most people go through life undergoing a series of happenings, which pass through their systems undigested. Happenings become experiences when they are digested, when they are reflected on, related to general patterns, and synthesized." – Saul Alinsky, *Rules for Radicals*

"Be honest about how much time you spend at work and why. Is it really necessary to work long, extra hours to accomplish your tasks and objectives, or are you regularly staying late for other reasons? To impress your boss and your peers, or simply because you are not managing your time well during the day?" – Gill Corkindale

"Remind yourself that you are much more than your job. However much you love your job, it is a mistake to define yourself too closely to your work. Take time to reflect on what you want to achieve in life and think about your definition of personal success." – Gill Corkindale

"Your life is a reflection of your choices. If you don't like what those choices have gotten you up to this point, suck it up and admit it, and then make different ones." – Paula Renaye

"The surest sign of the higher life is serenity. Moral progress results in freedom from inner turmoil. You can stop fretting about this and that."
– Epictetus

"Instead of nurturing your life purpose, you may have put it aside in the dark, closing the door on the idea that you can ever achieve fulfillment. When we have allowed ourselves to get smaller and smaller, we wind up living without the fullness of our being." – Carol Adrienne

"There is only one success, to be able to spend your life in your own way."
– Christopher Morley

"Some of the most forlorn people I know are those who haven't found their work....On the other side, people who have found their work can seem, while at work, creatures of great dignity, even beauty... The most fortunate people of all are those rare few for whom the line between work and play gets rubbed out and for whom work is pleasure and pleasure is work. I sometimes think that the world is divided between those who work so they can live and those who live chiefly so they can work." – Joseph Epstein

"Every calling is marked by a season of insignificance, a period when nothing seems to make sense. This is a time of wandering in the wilderness, when you feel alone and misunderstood. To the outsider, such a time looks like failure, as if you are grasping at air or simply wasting time. But the reality is this is the most important experience a person can have if they make the most of it." - Jeff Goins

"It's better to be a good person and fulfill your obligations than to have renown and power." –Epictetus

"Don't just tell your life what you want to do with it; listen to what it wants to do with you." – Parker Palmer

"We want work to offer us recognition and appreciation, the opportunity to be effective and to make a difference, the chance to really belong, but only rarely does any of this occur.....Work will remain for most of us a disutility – something that people do as a means to put bread on the table, not as an end...Too many of us come home at the end of the day feeling like the working wounded...Only a few of us feel engaged, energized, or ennobled by what we do. Most of us feel used rather than useful. .....It is utopian to think that we can love all our work. We cannot always find the perfect fit: sometimes the fit is fractured. But it is demeaning to think that we must separate labor and love. For work without love is servitude." – Al Gini

"When you want something, all the universe conspires in helping you to achieve it." – Paulo Coelho

Sweet Spot ~ Wish List ~ Fit Check ~ Work Crafting ~ Big Picture

- ☑ Find your sweet spot: Identify your current overall work-life balance and find your place of balance and peace.
- ☑ Create your Wish List: Determine what's important to you in terms of what brings meaning and joy, your unique strengths, and how you define success.
- ☑ Check for fit: Evaluate your current job through the lens of your Wish List.
- ☑ Craft your work: Redefine your current job so that it fits better with what's important to you.
- ☑ See the big picture: Put it all in perspective!

Tool 10 – Roxanne's Tips

1. Find your sweet spot.
   a) Create a ballpark estimate (high or low) of (a) how much time and energy you're investing in your work and (b) how meaningful it is to you. Is it high or low in both areas?
   b) Find the quadrant that best describes your current situation in the following Sweet Spot diagram and descriptions. Keep in mind that some jobs might fit into more than one quadrant.

	Meaning (high)		
	Q4 Coasting	Q3 Engaged	
Investment (low)	---	---	Investment (high)
	Q1 Disengaged	Q2 Hamster on a wheel	
	Meaning (low)		

   Let's look at what's happening in each quadrant:

   i. Quadrant 1 – Low meaning/low investment; Employees in this quadrant 'work to live' and are disengaged from their work. They're surviving the workplace, rather than thriving. Work is a means to an end. In other words, they do the work, but they don't let it interfere with their life. Work pays the bills so that they can do meaningful/fun things outside of work. In this way, work and life are segmented and separate. They mostly get meaning and joy from their personal lives. At work, they do what is necessary to reach the required performance standards. They try not to work overtime, think about work on off-hours, or bring work home. They experience little work stress, meaning, or satisfaction. Their reward is the money, time, and energy that it provides for their personal time.

ii. Quadrant 2 – Low meaning/high investment: For these folks, work crowds out and ~~flows~~ floods into their family and leisure time. The boundaries are diffuse. These employees focus on their work and are thinking about or doing work during non-work time. Overtime is common. More often than not, they may be striving or frenetically trying to make some headway on their excessive workload. However, the hamster wheel keeps spinning, and every day seems to run into the next day. Based on their high investment, it seems that they 'live to work' and have zero work-life balance. They aren't sure that they're accomplishing much of any long-term meaning, but there's lots of activity. They work very hard, but they're not feeling engaged or excited about their work. They don't get a lot of personal satisfaction or meaning from their work either. And, unlike their disengaged cousins in Q1, they experience tons of stress. They are far too exhausted to do much when they arrive home from work. They feel overinvested. They may identify with their work and feel consumed by it. They eat, sleep, and breathe their work. At the same time, some Q2 employees worry that, without work, their lives would be empty. Some might tell them to 'get a life.'

iii. Quadrant 3 – High meaning/High investment: Employees in this quadrant are fully engaged. They highly value their work and place it at the center of their lives. They invest lots of time and energy into their work, and they derive high levels of meaning and satisfaction from their work. They have the 'pedal to the metal,' and they're enjoying the ride. They believe that they're making a significant contribution, so their huge investment seems worth it. As in Q2, work may still be crowding out their personal life, but they're getting a reward in return for their investment.

iv. Quadrant 4 – High meaning/Low investment: Employees in this quadrant are probably unique, and some would say that they're lucky. Whatever little time and energy these folks invest in their work, they derive a great deal of meaning from it. Are they simply coasting and cherry-picking their tasks, so that they do only the ones that bring a sense of contribution? Perhaps, these folks are doing part-time work, consulting, or engaging in self-employed pursuits that are highly enjoyable and not too demanding. This reminds me (perhaps wrongly) of some FIRE advocates (Financial Independence Retire Early) who focus solely on rewarding pursuits such as blogging and gigs that capture their attention. I also wonder if minimalists Joshua and Ryan would be part of this quadrant (although I'm not sure how much time and energy they invest in pursuing their passions).

c) Now that you've figured out where you fit on the diagram, identify where you would like to be, ideally. This is your sweet spot: where you'll feel like you're thriving and fulfilled, and your work-life has just the right amount of balance for you. Each person has their sweet spot. For me (Roxanne), my sweet spot is where I get a lot of meaning from my work with a moderate level of investment (I'm in cruise control). It's where the star is on the diagram on the next page. This gives me a good deal of work/life balance.

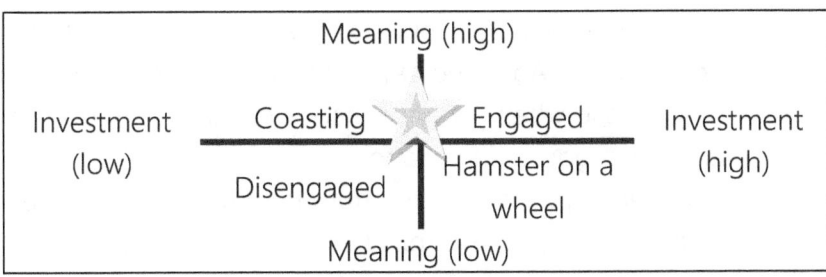

2. Create your Wish List. The previous step signaled where your overall life focus is. It's the broad pattern or big picture of the work/life balance that you want. Now, let's get down to specifics about what's important to you (your Wish List). Below are several approaches for doing this. Do any or all of them and stop when you have a crystal clear idea of your Wish List.

    a) 'Wow' experiences: Describe, in writing, three of your top work experiences in the past few years. As Tony Schwartz and Catherine McCarthy, both from The Energy Project, suggest, these are experiences during which you felt amazingly "effective, effortlessly absorbed, inspired, and fulfilled." They could be when you felt most 'alive,' successful, and had a sense of meaning and purpose. Next, review what you've written and highlight the keywords. Then, look for themes and patterns in the activities and the underlying talents and needs that were being drawn upon. Julie Mosow, *Harvard Business Review* author, suggests that you ask yourself what conditions allowed you to flourish. For example, perhaps you were given lots of autonomy, or you were allowed to be creative in finding solutions.

    b) Flow experiences: Similarly, describe, in writing, the last three times that you were in a state of flow (in other words, when time passed without your being aware of it). What were you doing? Carol Adrienne says, "You are almost always working on purpose when you lose track of time." Then do the same analysis suggested in a) above.

    c) Obstacle experiences: Describe, in writing, three experiences when you have felt blocked or highly frustrated. These experiences have lessons to teach us about what's important to us. In particular, Carol Adrienne says, "Some part of your purpose is also being served as you deal with obstacles and problems (resolving obstacles brings you great power and knowledge of a specific kind – necessary for your specific purpose)... A piece of your life purpose may be fulfilled by the knowing that results from pain, struggle, and illness...Generally, when you are on the right path, things flow. When you are attracting nothing but obstacles, you need to stop and ask yourself, 'What do I need to change in my thinking?'" Then do the same analysis suggested in a).

d) Biggest strengths: Describe, in writing: (a) What have you been complimented on by others? (b) What feels 'easy,' 'interesting,' and 'fun' for you? (c) What do you 'naturally' put energy into? (d) What do you most appreciate in others? Carol Adrienne suggests that "Your calling can also be glimpsed in what you admire in others. It can be seen in those abilities you have that you don't even think are special." (e) Carol Adrienne suggests that you ask yourself, "How would you describe yourself without referring to what you do for a living? ...What kind of work would you call 'too good to be true'? What do you do even if you don't get paid for it? Within these activities are the seeds of your passion...Follow through on persistent intuitive messages...Let synchronicities confirm that you are on the right path, even if their meaning is not crystal clear." Do the same analysis suggested in a).

e) Success definition: Success is a matter of different strokes for different folks. (a) Describe, in writing, your definition of success; in other words, what it takes for you to feel successful. (b) Now, place in priority order the following different sources of success identified by leadership guru James Clawson. We may have two rankings: (a) our 'actual' priority order, which reflects how much time we actually invest in each source of success, and (b) our 'aspired' priority order, which is what we see as being ideal.

Source of Success	Priority order	
	Actual	Aspired
Wealth (more money)		
Power (take control, make the rules)		
Fame (being well-known)		
Expertise (craftsmanship, talents, doing something very well)		
Salvation (being saved in the next life, spiritual depth, developing yourself and those around you)		
Health (sleep, diet, exercise, emotional stability)		
Happy family (spending lots of time interacting with family)		
Contribution to society (making a difference, working on important causes)		
Resonance/flow/feel (how you feel, for example: light, unhurried, and engaged)		

Now, analyze your results. Given your success priorities, how would you rewrite your definition of success? A final note, James Clawson has two big lessons to teach us about success. First, he says that "what you love you'll do, and what you do is a reflection of what you love." In other words, if you truly value something, it will show in the number of hours that you devote to it. Regarding wealth, James Clawson cautions us about the 'happiness set point' beyond which more money doesn't result in greater happiness. Indeed, James Clawson says that "Many religious traditions have long since figured this out (why seeking more money or power never satisfies) and argue that the path to happiness and serenity is to renounce the material world."

f) Design your Wish List: Based on the patterns or themes that you discovered in exercises a) to e), summarize the key elements that you desire in your work (in other words, what brings meaning, your strengths, your success elements, etc.). For example, one element might be: "Creativity – I apply creative, unique, and inventive solutions to problems."

	Element	Description
1		
2		
3		
4		
5		
6		
7		
8		
9		
10		

3. Check for fit:
   a) What does your current job look like? Complete the following "Current Job Map." Place each of your current job tasks in the applicable quadrant. Provide enough detail on the diagram to permit another person to understand your job from it. (By the way, when you did the Vital Few Exercise in Tool 6, you identified the three most vital things that you can do to help you feel like you've had a super productive day, and you figured out ways to do these as efficiently as possible. You might find it helpful to look back at your notes for that exercise.)

Current Job Map

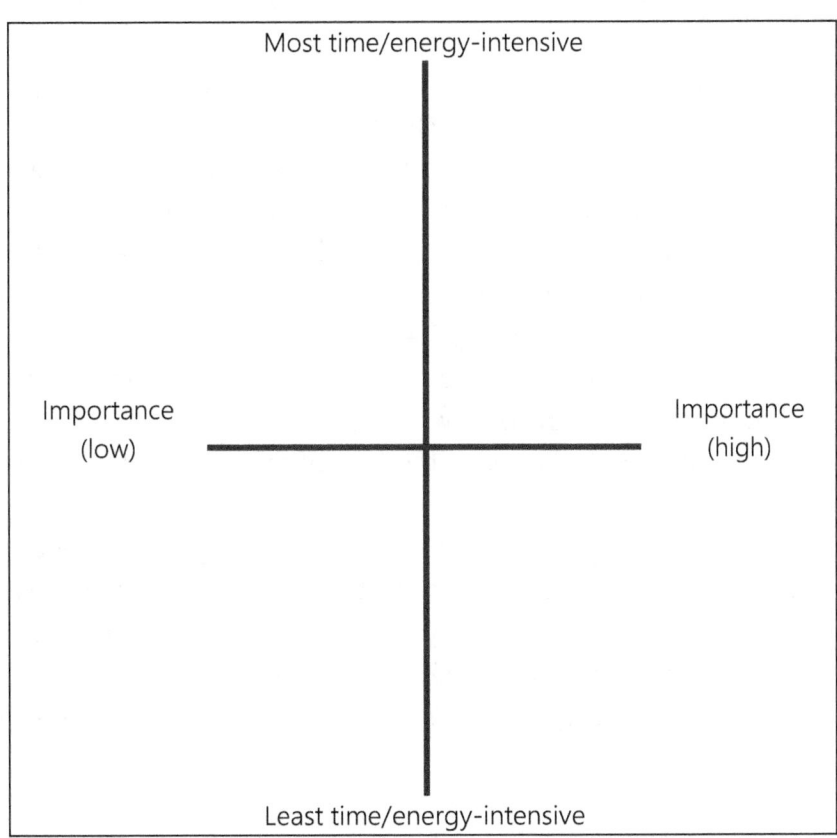

b) Analyze your current job for fit. Now comes a crucial part: analyzing your current job through the lens of your Wish List. Circle tasks on your Current Job Map that meet any of the items from your Wish List. Let's say that you have 'Creativity' on your Wish List; you would circle any task that meets your need for creativity. Next, place a number beside the task that represents how well it fits with items on your Wish List. For example, if my task "Providing Client Training" fulfills items 1 and 2 on my Wish List, I would circle the task and write 1 and 2 in the circle.

c) Identify the big gaps. This is where you look at the strengths and weaknesses of the fit between your Wish List and your Current Job Map.
  i. What Wish List items are not addressed (or only rarely so) by your Current Job Map?
  ii. What tasks are not circled? (These are targets for elimination or modification.)
  iii. What are the three biggest gaps? (These can be issues, potential for improvement, concerns, etc.)
  iv. What conclusions can you draw from your analysis?
  v. How do you feel about the results of your analysis? Why? Did anything surprise you?

4. Craft your work. In this part, you redefine your job so that it's better aligned with your Wish List.
  a) Consider your options for each of the three gaps that you just identified:
    i. Can you eliminate poorly fitting tasks altogether, delegate them, or swap them with someone else? How?
    ii. Can you reduce your time and energy investment in poorly fitting tasks (for example, by changing their frequency or scope) so that your focus is on better-fitting tasks? How?

      iii. Can you change how you carry out poorly fitting tasks to make them more meaningful (for example, enriching or enlarging them)?

      iv. Can you create bundles or groupings of tasks that are more aligned with your Wish List? How?

      v. Can you reframe them to make them more meaningful? How? For example, instead of 'attending boring team meetings,' perhaps you can use these meetings as a time to connect with or learn from colleagues.

      vi. Can you add new tasks that would help you fulfill your Wish List? How?

NOTE: Don't automatically answer "No" to all of these questions. You may have more latitude to make changes than you think.

FOR HUGE GAPS: Was there absolutely no fit between your Wish List and your Current Job Map? In other words, does it seem impossible to optimize your current job so that it aligns with your needs? This is an 'unfortunate truth' for some individuals. If this is your case, this may be an important decision time for you: do you stay with your job, hoping to fill the gaps even partially so that your joy and peace don't dribble out, eventually leaving you feeling numb, or do you 'face reality' and look for a job (or something else) where there's a better fit? Only _you_ can answer that question for yourself.

b) Now what? After having brainstormed possible options for addressing the gaps, choose the solutions that are likely to have the highest impact on you.

      i. Revise your Current Job Map to see how it would change if you implemented your selected solutions. You might create an Optimized Job Map that reflects your 'new and improved' tasks (and the Wish List items that they fit with). By the way, if you still have unimportant tasks that you're investing lots of time in, you may want to rethink your new map!

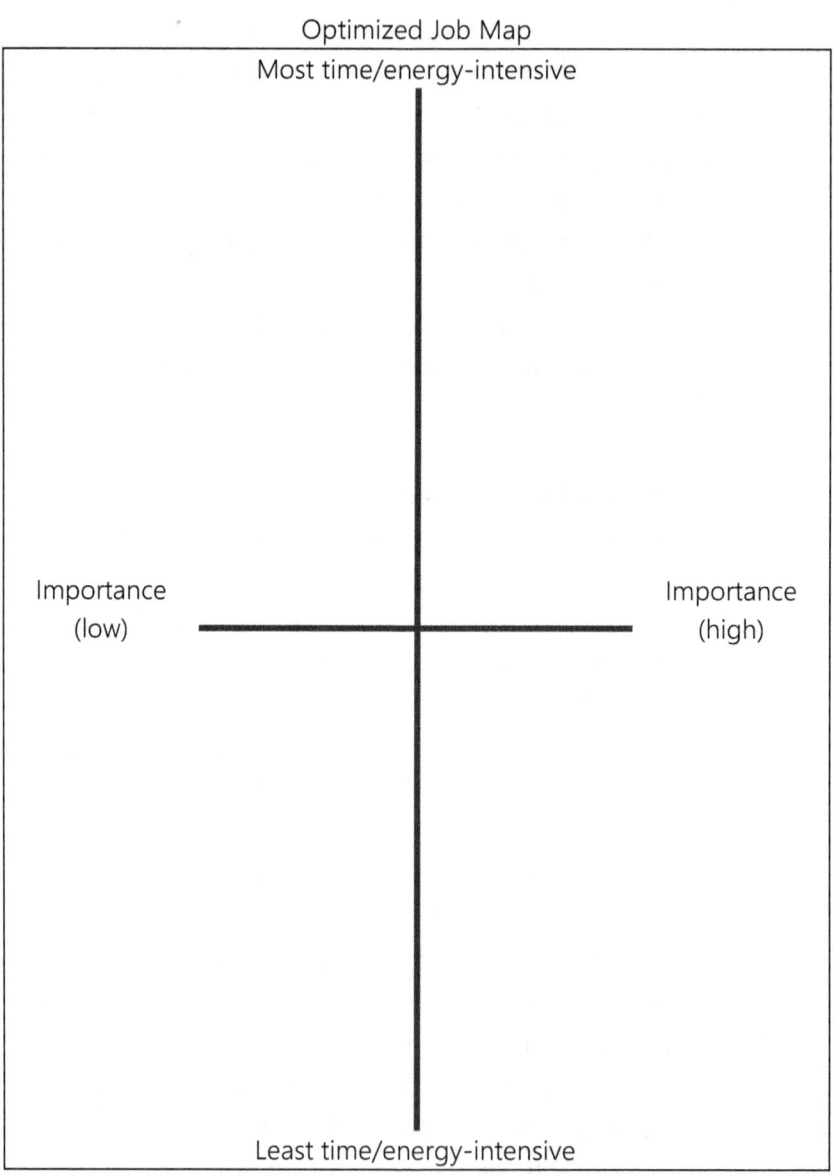

ii. Next, fill in the Gaps/Solutions Table below. This is your implementation plan. Then, of course, implement your plan!

Gap/Solutions Table

Gap	Solution	Action steps (include deadlines)	Possible challenges & ways to overcome them
1		a.	
		b.	
		c.	
2		d.	
		e.	
		f.	
3		g.	
		h.	
		i.	

5. See the big picture.
    a) Adjust your perception of what it means to be successful. Do you think that you're not successful unless you get regular promotions and increasing responsibility? Please realize that promotions aren't necessary to experience success on the job. Each of us has our personal vision of success. For some, it's a prestigious position, possessing a considerable fortune, or achieving fame and glory. For others, it's about having an interesting job that aligns with their values, having satisfying relationships with others, or making a difference in society. According to researchers Laura Nash and Howard Stevenson, success is found in the four areas of life (self, family, work, and community) and has four components:
        i. Happiness: your level of fulfillment and satisfaction in your daily life and surroundings.
        ii. Achievement: the sum of your accomplishments that make you feel proud and that represent your involvement and efforts.
        iii. Significance: the positive influence that you have on the people around you.
        iv. Legacy: your impact or the way that your accomplishments inspire others to seek personal success.

    In their research, Nash and Stevenson found that the most successful people "focused on creating a well-balanced big picture" by adding new activities for all components in all the areas of their life. In other words, they didn't put all of their eggs in one basket. Just as in relationships, if you expect to get all of your needs met from one person or activity (or job, for that matter), you will be sorely disappointed.

    b) Beware of spending your life chasing happiness. Once you reach a level of success that you think will make you happy, your goalposts might change, and happiness may become a moving target! You think you'll be happy when you earn "x" amount, but when you reach that level, you change your goal

to "x + 20%. This is a guaranteed way of being unhappy with your life. Indeed, Ron Rolheiser, former president of the Oblate School of Theology in San Antonio, Texas, cautions that striving for happiness can be futile because life is never a perfect bed of roses. For him, looking for meaning in our lives is more important because "We have a false, over-idealized, and unrealistic concept of happiness. We tend to equate happiness with two things: pleasure and lack of tension. Hence, we fantasize that for us to be happy, we would need to be in a situation where we are free of all the tensions that normally flood into our lives. But that isn't what constitutes happiness. Meaning is what constitutes happiness, and meaning isn't contingent upon pain and tension being absent from our lives." In other words, we can lead amazing lives full of meaning, even though we're not perfectly happy.

c) Live inside-out lives (be confident, self-expressive, self-driven, and authentic without being selfish). Don't be a passive observer of your life or allow circumstances and others to determine your speed and direction. According to well-known leadership researcher James Clawson, many people live outside-in. They feel restless, incomplete, and disconnected. They "hesitate and censor who they are to fit in with those around them. ...We need a willingness to conform to create a viable society. But if we live too much outside-in, we lose our individuality and our capacity not only to lead but to live our own lives and to manage our careers." At its extreme, an outside-inner is a doormat with very little agency. How sad!

d) We become our work (so choose well). In his classic book, *My Job, My Self*, Al Gina emphasizes this idea repeatedly. He says, "Work is the way we come to know the world and are known to the world. Work becomes our mark of identity, our signature on the world. ...Because work preoccupies our lives and is the central focus of our time and energies, it not only provides us with an income, but it also literally names us, identifies us, to both ourselves and others...Although different kinds of work affect different people differently, every person's self-portrait is both directly and indirectly influenced by the work that they do. Some of our job-acquired characteristics and behavioral patterns are substantial and life-altering."

e) Remember that we are more than our jobs. We shouldn't have our identity and sense of personal value all wrapped up in our work. One December, I (Roxanne) lost my job, and as I was watching the mall Santa Claus hugging children, I felt worthless. I envied this man, who (I was told) was an unemployed guy who was very happy to snag the Santa Claus job. Frankly, I felt embarrassed. "Who am I?" I would ask myself. Without a job, I didn't know who I was. It took me some time to realize that I was much more than my job. I had value and was contributing to the people around me in my personal life, despite not having a job.

f) Think bigger. Look beyond ordinary day-to-day concerns and consider your larger purpose in life: how you can make a difference in the lives of others. As Jeff Goins says in his book, "What we all want is to know our time on earth has meant something. We can distract ourselves with pleasure for only so long before beginning to wonder what the point is. This means if we want true satisfaction, we have to rise above the pettiness of our own desires and do what is required of us." In other words, we shouldn't settle for or accept a crappy situation (perhaps out of fear of the unknown or a lack of courage to step out of our comfort zone). Jeff Goins says that, if we do so, "No matter how noisy the world got, no matter how busy you became, there would always be something inside you — a small voice that whispered in the quieter moments of life, taunting you with the shadow of the unlived life. If you listen hard enough, you can still hear it." Is there something that you're unhappy about that has been dragging on for a while?

6. Consider the lessons of the Mexican fisherman story (written by Heinrich Böll):

An investment banker was vacationing in a coastal Mexican village when he saw a small boat with several fish in it. The banker, impressed by the quality of the fish, asked the fisherman how long it took to catch them.

"Only a little while," the fisherman replied.

"Why don't you stay out longer and catch more fish?" the banker asked.

"Because I have enough to support my family's needs," the fisherman replied.

"But what do you do with the rest of your time?"
"I sleep late, fish a little, play with my children, take a siesta with my wife, stroll into the village each evening where I sip wine and play guitar with my amigos. Life is good, señor."

"I'm an Ivy League MBA, and I can help you. If you spend more time fishing and buy a bigger boat with the proceeds, then with the proceeds from the bigger boat, you could buy several boats until eventually, you will have a whole fleet of fishing boats. Instead of selling your catch to the middleman, you could sell directly to the processor, eventually opening your own cannery. You could control the product, processing, and distribution. Of course, you would need to leave this small coastal fishing village and move to Mexico City, where you would run your growing enterprise."

"But señor, how long will this all take?"

"15-20 years."

"But what then, señor?"

"That's the best part. When the time is right, you would announce an IPO and sell your company stock to the public and make millions."

"Millions, señor? Then what?"

"Then you would retire. You could move to a small coastal fishing village where you would sleep late, fish a little, play with your kids, take a siesta with your wife, stroll to the village in the evenings where you could sip wine and play your guitar with your amigos."

Final Thoughts

This book offers you some tools that allow you to achieve a sense of meaning, peace, and joy at work and leave behind habits that don't work. You can continue growing and learning by paying attention to your personal experiences, failures, and successes. What are they telling you?

Even though we watch others succeed and make mistakes, learning from someone else's lessons can be challenging. Over time, you must build your personal toolkit or user's manual of what works and what doesn't work for you.

Keep in mind that you might meet up with some resistance along your journey toward minimalism. Resistance is a natural part of change. Some people won't like the fact that you're doing things unconventionally ("Why can't you be normal?"), that you're charting your own path ("You're ruffling feathers by not just going along with what everyone else is doing."), or that you're feeling good about your work life ("You're making us look bad."). Please don't accept these invitations to feel bad. Whether their source is jealousy, insecurity, or something else, you are 'the boss of you,' and you get to make your own choices. Simply smile and know that you're on the right path!

Good luck with the rest of your journey!

~ ~ ~

References

Achor, Shaun (2018). *The Happiness Advantage: How a Positive Brain Fuels Success in Work and Life*. Currency.

Adrienne, Carol (1998). *The Purpose of Your Life*. Eagle Brook.

Baumeister, R. F., & Leary, M. R. (1995). The need to belong: Desire for interpersonal attachments as a fundamental human motivation. *Psychological Bulletin, 117*(3), 497-529.

Bloem, Craig (2018). *Why successful people wear the same thing every day*. Retrieved from: https://www.inc.com/craig-bloem/this-1-unusual-habit-helped-make-mark-zuckerberg-steve-jobs-dr-dre-successful.html

Berg, Justin; Dutton, Jane & Wrzesniewski, Amy (2013). Job crafting and meaningful work. In Bryan Dik, Zinta Byrne, & Michael Steger (Editors). *Purpose and Meaning in the Workplace*. American Psychological Association.

Burns, David (2008). *Feeling Good: The New Mood Therapy*. Harper.

Carver, Courtney (2010). *Project 333*. Retrieved from: https://bemorewithless.com/project-333/

CBC News (2016). *Coquitlam Mayor Richard Stewart wore same suit for 15 months and nobody noticed*. Retrieved from: https://www.cbc.ca/news/canada/british-columbia/coquitlam-richard-stewart-suit-1.3459469

Center for Studies on Human Stress (Centre d'Études sur le stress humain) (undated). Recette du stress. Retrieved from http://www.stresshumain.ca/le-stress/comprendre-son-stress/source-du-stress.html

Chan, Jennifer (2018). *5 Ways Practicing "Mental Minimalism" has Tangibly Improved my Life*. Retrieved from: https://thefinancialdiet.com/tk-ways-minimalism-has-honestly-improved-my-life/

Chismar, Douglas (2001). Vice and virtue in everyday (business) life. *Journal of Business Ethics*, *29*(1-2), 169-176.

Clawson, James. (2009). *Balancing Your Life: Executive Lessons for Work, Family and Self*. World Scientific.

Corkindale, Gill (2011). Detach yourself from your work. *Harvard Business Review*. Retrieved from: https://hbr.org/2011/01/detach-yourself-from-your-work

Covey, Stephen (1993). *The Seven Habits of Highly Effective People*. Simon and Schuster.

Covey, Stephen (1992). *Principle-Centered Leadership*. Simon and Schuster.

Culp, S. (1991). *Streamlining Your Life: A 5-point Plan for Uncomplicated Living*. Writers Digest Books.

Crestani, Belinda (2017). *Eight Simple Ways to Clear Mental Clutter*. Retrieved from: https://www.acuitymag.com/business/eight-simple-ways-to-clear-mental-clutter

Dhand, Rajiv & Sohal, Harjyot (2007). Good sleep, bad sleep! The role of daytime naps in healthy adults. *Current Opinion in Internal Medicine. 6: 91.*

Driver, Mike (1979). Career concepts and career management in organizations. In Cooper, Cary (Editor). *Behavioral Problems in Organizations*, Principe Hall.

Duke, Kristen; Ward, Adrian; Gneezy, Avelet; & Bos, Maarten (2018). *Harvard Business Review*. Retrieved from: https://hbr.org/2018/03/ having-your-smartphone-nearby-takes-a-toll-on-your-thinking

Dweck, Carol (2007). *Mindset: The New Psychology of Success.* Ballantine Books.

Ferriss, Timothy (2009). *The 4-hour workweek.* Expanded and Updated, With Over 100 New Pages of Cutting-Edge Content. Harmony.

Gazzaley, Adam & Rosen, Larry (2016). *The Distracted Mind: Ancient Brains in a High-Tech World.* MIT Press.

Gini, Al (2013). *My Job, My Self: Work and the Creation of the Modern Individual.* Routledge.

Goins, Jeff (2015). *The Art of Work: A Proven Path to Discovering What You Were Meant to Do.* Nelson Books.

Gottman, John, & Levenson, Robert (2000). The timing of divorce: Predicting when a couple will divorce over a 14-year period. *Journal of Marriage and Family, 62*(3), 737-745.

Grant, Adam (2013). *Give and Take.* Viking.

Honoré, Carl. (2009). *In Praise of Slow: How a Worldwide Movement is Challenging the Cult of Speed.* Vintage Canada.

Jaffee, Dennis & Scott, Cynthia (1984). *From Burnout to Balance: A Workbook for Peak Performance and Self-Renewal.* McGraw-Hill.

Johnson, Adam (2012). The new duck metaphor. *The Stanford Daily.* Retrieved from: https://www.stanforddaily.com/2012/09/26/the-new-duck-metaphor/

Juran, Joseph (1992). *Juran on Quality by Design: The New Steps for Planning Quality into Goods and Services.* Simon and Schuster.

Kabat-Zinn, John (2009). *Wherever You Go, There You Are: Mindfulness Meditation in Everyday Life.* Hachette Books.

Klein, André (undated). *Minimalism: Spiritual Materialism in Disguise or: The New Religion of "Living with 100 things."* Retrieved from: https://learnoutlive.com/minimalism-spiritual-materialism-in-disguise-or-the-new-religion-of-living-with-100-things/

Kondō, Marie (2014). *The Life-Changing Magic of Tidying Up: The Japanese Art of Decluttering and Organizing.* Random House Canada.

Lahl, Olaf; Wispel, Christiane; Willigens, Bernadette; & Pietrowsky, Reinhard (2008). An ultra-short episode of sleep is sufficient to promote declarative memory performance. *Journal of Sleep Research. 17*(1): 3–10.

Mandel, Phillip (undated). *Count Yourself to Sleep.* Retrieved from: http://www.magicwandcoach.com/count-to-sleep.htm

Mann, Merlin (2007). *Inbox Zero.* GoogleTechTalks. Retrieved from: https://www.youtube.com/watch?v=z9UjeTMb3Yk

McCloud, Cloud (2016). *Have You Filled a Bucket Today? 10th Anniversary Edition: A Guide to Daily Happiness for Kids.* Brighton, MI: Bucket Fillers, Inc.

McMains, Stephanie & Kastner, Sabine (2011). Interactions of top-down and bottom-up mechanisms in human visual cortex. *Journal of Neuroscience, 31*(2), 587-59

Mellon, Andrew (2012). *The organizational triangle©.* Retrieved from: https://www.andrewmellen.com/organizational-triangle/

Millburn, Joshua Fields & Nicodemus, Ryan (2014). *Everything that Remains: A Memoir by the Minimalists.* Asymmetrical Press.

Millburn, Joshua Fields & Nicodemus, Ryan (2015). *Minimalism: Live a Meaningful Life.* Asymmetrical Press.

Millburn, Joshua Fields & Nicodemus, Ryan (undated). *Podcast 157: Excess.* Retrieved from: https://www.theminimalists.com/podcast/

Mischel, W. (2014). *The Marshmallow Test: Understanding Self-Control and How to Master it.* Random House.

Mosow, Julie (2014). How to motivate yourself when your boss doesn't. *Harvard Business Review.* Retrieved from: https://hbr.org/2014/11/how-to-motivate-yourself-when-your-boss-doesnt

Nash, Laura & Stevenson, Howard (2004). Success that lasts. *Harvard Business Review, 82*(2), 102-109. Retrieved from https://hbr.org/2004/02/success-that-lasts

National Institute of Mental Health (2002). 'Power nap' prevents burnout; morning sleep perfects a skill. *Science Daily.* Retrieved from: https://www.sciencedaily.com/releases/2002/07/020702065823.htm

Oncken, William & Wass, Donald (1974). Management time: Who's got the monkey? *Harvard Business Review.* Retrieved from: http://www.mcrhrdi.gov.in/91fc/coursematerial/management/17%20Who%20Has%20Got%20The%20Monkey.pdf

Ophir, Eyal; Nass, Clifford & Wagner, Anthony (2009). Cognitive control in media multitaskers. *Proceedings of the National Academy of Sciences, 106*(37), 15583-15587.

Oppezzo, Marily & Schwartz, Daniel (2014). Give your ideas some legs: The positive effect of walking on creative thinking. *Journal of Experimental Psychology: Learning, Memory, and Cognition, 40*(4), 1142.

Porcellino, John. (2008). *Thoreau at Walden.* The Center for Cartoon Studies. Disney Book Group.

Poupard, D. (2003). À l'encontre du stress, de la fatigue et de l'épuisement, une vie pleinement saine!

Ravikant, Naval (2017). Naval Ravikant on reading, happiness, systems for decision making, habits, honesty and more. Retrieved from https://www.farnamstreetblog.com/2017/02/naval-ravikant-reading-decision-making/

Renaye, Paula (2012). *Living the Life You Love*. Diomo Books.

Rolheiser, Ron (2011). Meaning and happiness. Retrieved from http://ronrolheiser.com/meaning-and--happiness/#WN9lpWyvIV

Rosen, Larry (2018). 5 ways to counteract your smartphone addiction. *Harvard Business Review*. Retrieved from: https://hbr.org/2018/03/5-ways-to-counteract-your-smartphone-addiction

Russo, Marcello; Ollier-Malaterre, Arianne & Morandin, Gabriele (2019). If you want to use your phone less, first figure out why. *Harvard Business Review*. Retrieved from: https://hbr.org/2019/06/if-you-want-to-use-your-phone-less-first-figure-out-why

Schwartz, Tony & McCarthy, Catherine (2007). Manage your energy, not your time. *Harvard Business Review*. Retrieved from: https://hbr.org/2007/10/manage-your-energy-not-your-time

Scott, Elizabeth (2019). *How to Develop an Internal Locus of Control*. Retrieved from: https://www.verywellmind.com/develop-an internal-locus-of-control-3144943

Small, Laura (2018). Minimalism for work: How 'less is more' can help your professional life. Retrieved from: https://smartbrief.com/original/2018/03/minimalism-work-how-less-more-can-help-your-professional-life

Thompson, Jody & Ressler, Cali (2013). *Why Managing Sucks and How to fix it: A Results-Only Guide to Taking Control of Work, not People*. Wiley.

Tracy, Brian (2017). *Eat that Frog! 21 Great Ways to Stop Procrastinating and Get More Done in Less Time.* Berrett-Koehler Publishers.

Weil, Andrew (undated). The 4-7-8 (or Relaxing Breath) Exercise. Retrieved from: https://www.drweil.com/health-wellness/body-mind-spirit/stress-anxiety/breathing-three-exercises/

Weisbord, Marvin (1987). *Productive Workplaces: Organizing for Dignity, Meaning, and Community.* Jossey-Bass.

Whitfield, Charles (1993). *Boundaries and Relationships: Knowing, Protecting and Enjoying the Self.* Health Communications, Inc.

ABOUT THE AUTHOR

Céleste Grimard holds a PhD in Organizational Behavior and is certified in Reality Therapy. As a professor, she loves inspiring learners to grow into effective leaders, managers, and employees. Her research looks at the human side of work, exploring emotions, burnout, and workplace bullying.

Beyond the ivory tower, you might find her doting on a super-cute black pug, playing pickleball with friends, or nurturing her spiritual life through acts of service and quiet contemplation.

She has written numerous books, available on Amazon, and academic articles, which can be found through Google Scholar. A lifelong book lover, both as a reader and a writer, she cherishes meaningful conversations, laughter, and the simple joy of connecting with people.

www.ingramcontent.com/pod-product-compliance
Lightning Source LLC
Chambersburg PA
CBHW060855170526
45158CB00001B/361